C000093573

Behavior-Driven Development with Cucumber

Behavior-Driven Development with Cucumber

Better Collaboration for Better Software

Richard Lawrence
with Paul Rayner

✦✦ Addison-Wesley

Boston • Columbus • New York • San Francisco • Amsterdam • Cape Town • Dubai
London • Madrid • Milan • Munich • Paris • Montreal • Toronto • Delhi • Mexico City
São Paulo • Sydney • Hong Kong • Seoul • Singapore • Taipei • Tokyo

Many of the designations used by manufacturers and sellers to distinguish their products are claimed as trademarks. Where those designations appear in this book, and the publisher was aware of a trademark claim, the designations have been printed with initial capital letters or in all capitals.

The authors and publisher have taken care in the preparation of this book, but make no expressed or implied warranty of any kind and assume no responsibility for errors or omissions. No liability is assumed for incidental or consequential damages in connection with or arising out of the use of the information or programs contained herein.

For information about buying this title in bulk quantities, or for special sales opportunities (which may include electronic versions; custom cover designs; and content particular to your business, training goals, marketing focus, or branding interests), please contact our corporate sales department at corpsales@pearsoned.com or (800) 382-3419.

For government sales inquiries, please contact governmentsales@pearsoned.com.

For questions about sales outside the U.S., please contact intlcs@pearson.com.

Visit us on the Web: informit.com/aw

Library of Congress Control Number: 2019937018

Copyright © 2019 Pearson Education, Inc.

All rights reserved. This publication is protected by copyright, and permission must be obtained from the publisher prior to any prohibited reproduction, storage in a retrieval system, or transmission in any form or by any means, electronic, mechanical, photocopying, recording, or likewise. For information regarding permissions, request forms and the appropriate contacts within the Pearson Education Global Rights & Permissions Department, please visit www.pearsoned.com/permissions/.

ISBN-13: 978-0-321-77263-3
ISBN-10: 0-321-77263-6

Cover photograph © Food Travel Stockforlife/Shutterstock

Publisher
Mark L. Taub

Acquisitions Editor
Haze Humbert

Development Editor
Ellie Bru

Managing Editor
Sandra Schroeder

Senior Project Editor
Tonya Simpson

Indexer
Erika Millen

Proofreader
Abigail Manheim

Technical Reviewers
Leslie Brooks
Matt Heuser
Nicole Forsythe
Matt Wynne

Cover Designer
Chuti Prasertsith

Compositor
codeMantra

Contents

Acknowledgments

Writing this book was far and away the most difficult professional challenge I've ever undertaken. The book would not exist without the help and support of many people in my life.

I'm grateful to my business partner at Agile For All, Bob Hartman, for believing I had something to say on this topic that was worth a book and for getting the ball rolling on it.

Bob introduced me to Chris Guzikowski at Pearson, who took a risk on a new author and showed remarkable patience when client work often got in the way of writing.

I'm thankful for my friend Paul Rayner, who stepped in for a time as co-author when the book was stalled and helped transform it to be much more interesting and useful. Even after leaving the project to focus on other things, Paul still read drafts and offered invaluable feedback.

My wife, Dawn, provided endless patience and support throughout this long project. She read drafts, talked through ideas and challenges with me, and most of all sustained me with unwavering belief that I actually could see the project through. Thank you, Dawn.

My dad, Tom Lawrence, introduced me to software development as a child. He encouraged me and helped me grow early in my career. And then he was willing to take my ideas, apply them in his work, and help me make them better. To be able to become a peer and even a coach to the man who inspired me to do this work at all is a remarkable thing, and I'm so grateful for it.

I'm thankful to the many people who were willing to read unpolished drafts and sacrifice time to contribute detailed feedback. Thank you, Ingram Monk, Kim Barnes, Colin Deady, Dan Sharp, Sean Miller, Jen Dineen, David Madouros, Josh Adams, David Watson, Seb Rose, Aslak Hellesøy, Brennan Lawrence, Donna Hungarter, Nicole Forsythe, Matt Heusser, Matt Wynne, and Leslie Brooks. (And apologies to anyone I missed in that list—so many people read bits of the book over the eight years we worked on it.)

This is a book rather than just a bunch of words sitting on my computer because of the many great people at my publisher, Pearson. Thank you to Chris Zahn, Payal Sharotri, Mark Taub, Haze Humbert, and all those behind the scenes who I'll never interact with directly. Special thanks to my development editor Ellie Bru and copyeditor Tonya Simpson for carefully reading the book multiple times and helping me get the thoughts clear and the words just right.

My Agile For All colleagues have been encouraging, patient, and supportive. I'm thankful to work with such an amazing group of people.

I'm indebted to many in the BDD and Agile Testing communities who have shaped my thinking on these topics, including Ward Cunningham, Kent Beck, Ron Jeffries, Dan North, Liz Keogh, Matt Wynne, Aslak Hellesøy, Seb Rose, Gaspar Nagy, Lisa Crispin, Dale Emery, Elisabeth Hendrickson, Gojko Adzic, and Jerry Weinberg.

Finally, a huge thank you to my clients who have tried, challenged, and often extended my ideas. I learn from you every time we work together.

—Richard Lawrence

About the Authors

Richard Lawrence is co-owner of the consulting firm Agile For All. He trains and coaches people to collaborate more effectively with other people to solve complex, meaningful problems. He draws on a diverse background in software development, engineering, anthropology, and political science.

Richard was an early adopter of behavior-driven development and led the development of the first .NET version of Cucumber, Cuke4Nuke. He is a popular speaker at conferences on BDD and Agile software development.

Paul Rayner co-founded and co-leads DDD Denver. He regularly speaks at local user groups and at regional and international conferences. If you are looking for an expert hands-on team coach and design mentor in domain-driven design (DDD), BDD with Cucumber, or lean/agile processes, Paul is available for consulting and training through his company, Virtual Genius LLC.

Chapter 1

Focusing on Value

This book is about the practices and skills that get a team collaborating every day to build the right software in small slices, a set of practices known as behavior-driven development, or BDD. Building on the work of BDD pioneers Dan North and Liz Keogh, we define BDD as

- Exploring desired system behavior with examples in conversations
- Formalizing examples into automated tests to guide development

Most resources for those who want to learn to practice BDD with Cucumber focus on the test automation part of BDD. Some of that emphasis is due to the fact that most of the tools associated with BDD—tools like Cucumber—help with the formalization and automation parts of BDD. That, after all, is where you need software tools the most.

In our coaching, however, we've noticed that teams need the most help with the collaboration part of BDD, the part where the least help is available. Once teams learn how to explore changes in system behavior with examples in a series of conversations and to capture those examples in expressive language, automating those examples turns out to be relatively easy.

This book shares what we've seen work best for the collaboration side of BDD. We show how the collaboration flows into automation—you'll learn enough to get started automating your examples with Cucumber—but we haven't written a cookbook for automating tests with Cucumber. *This is a BDD book that uses Cucumber rather than a Cucumber book that mentions BDD.*

This emphasis is consistent with the Agile values. The first value statement in the Manifesto for Agile Software Development says, "We value individuals and interactions over processes and tools."[1] We first determine who needs to be involved and how they need to work together, and then we consider what processes and tools would support and amplify those interactions. Starting with a process or a tool easily leads to suboptimal results. So, before focusing on Cucumber, a tool, it makes sense for us to explore and understand the interactions Cucumber is designed to support.

BDD uses examples rather than abstract specifications to explore the future behavior of a system. In the same way, we're going to use examples to illustrate the BDD way of collaborating rather than just talking about it in theory. Throughout the book, we observe as the software development team for a (fictitious) large public library gets started with BDD. This will make it easier to see how BDD can help your team and to anticipate what it might look like for your team to adopt this way of working together.

The best way to understand the BDD way of collaborating, of course, is to experience it yourself. Beginning in Chapter 2, "Exploring with Examples," we suggest an approach to slowly and safely begin experimenting with BDD on your team. But first, we need to lay the foundation to get started.

In this chapter, our library team—and you—learn how to start a new initiative with a meaningful increment of value, which is an essential prerequisite for BDD.

Our Story Begins

Initial Conversation Between Mark and Susan

SUSAN: An executive at the library, responsible for all IT projects. Originally a librarian.

MARK: The software team's product owner, has worked for the public library for 8 years in various roles; knows the business domain well but has limited experience in software development.

Setting: The espresso bar at the main branch of the library

(As MARK pays for his order, he notices SUSAN waiting for her drink at the end of the bar.)

MARK: Susan, how's it going?

SUSAN: Good. I just got back last night from LibTech, the big library technology conference.

MARK: Pick up anything interesting there?

SUSAN: Actually, I did. You know how we were planning to finally start offering ebooks with the new budget this year?

(MARK nods.)

SUSAN: Well, I asked around and found that pretty much everybody hates the big off-the-shelf digital collection systems. It's nice that they handle the licensing with the publishers, but the user experience is horrible for the library staff and the patrons. And the license fees are pretty steep.

MARK: Maybe we should do our own system and do it right.

SUSAN: I was thinking about that. But how do we make sure we don't spend millions of dollars making a system to provide ebooks that has all the same problems? We could just buy one people hate. *(Grins)*

MARK: Hmm.

SUSAN: Can we do it in a way that gets people using it and giving us feedback before we dump our whole budget into this?

MARK: The Scrum approach my teams have been using certainly gives us a way to deliver more often. But we've still been treating projects as one big effort, even though we're working in small sprints. So, we're not getting the kind of early feedback you're talking about.

I wonder…There's a guy I met at a charity golf event last month who helps organizations deliver value and get feedback from software in a much more incremental way. His name's Jonah. Maybe he can work with us on this.

SUSAN: It's worth a try. Why don't you set up a meeting for the three of us in my office?

When Scrum Isn't Enough

Many teams go through the mechanics of something like Scrum but don't actually have potentially shippable product increments at the end of each sprint, let alone during the sprint. They simply lay sprints and Scrum meetings over their work as they've always done it.

Most teams who adopt an Agile approach to their work do so because they want to get progress, feedback, and value earlier and more often. A process framework like Scrum provides a good structure for this—planning and reviewing work in short cycles, frequently inspecting and adapting the process, and working from a prioritized backlog are all essential. But for most teams, there are some missing skills that keep them from getting the results they want. Our aim is to teach you these skills. Throughout this book, we'll see what it looks like for Mark and his team to learn this new way of working and how you can apply it to your own work.

Mark's team has been using Scrum like many organizations do at first: They commit to big projects, with detailed scope in a requirements document, just like they did before Scrum. They convert these requirements into a product backlog, per Scrum, but early sprints don't really deliver potentially shippable product increments. Instead, early sprints are heavy on architecture, infrastructure, design, and planning, with limited value for users.

Of course, all this back-end work needs testing. But until developers finally start exposing the back-end code via user-facing functionality, testers struggle to test it. Testers find themselves underused in early sprints and overwhelmed in later sprints.

The experience is similar for business stakeholders and users. Early in a project, there isn't much to see and to provide feedback on. Later, there's an overwhelming amount of stuff to look at and too little time to look at it.

Eventually, on every project it becomes clear that the team isn't going to hit the deadline for the required scope, so they either move the date or look for places to cut features or alter the overall scope. Unfortunately, many features that could be cut are already partially implemented, and some of the most essential features might not have been implemented yet at all.

Susan is right to be concerned that the ebook project would use up the whole budget without delivering something markedly better than the off-the-shelf alternative. Working the same way tends to produce the same results.

Some Scrum teams learn how to write user stories to capture small, but complete, slices of functionality. However, unless product owners, developers, and testers fundamentally change how they collaborate with each other, they still end up with a mini-waterfall in each sprint, as shown in Figure 1-1.

The first step in breaking out of mini- (or full-scale) waterfalls is to find a meaningful, but small, increment of value to begin with. Then, BDD can help teams grow a system example by example, planning, building, and testing every day.

Stories are small
enough to fit six
in the sprint...

...but four started
right away.

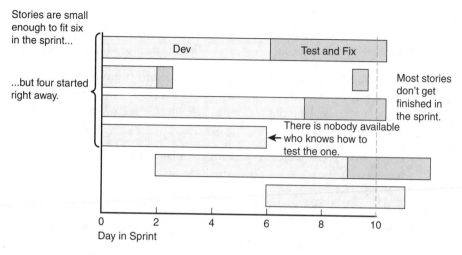

Most stories
don't get
finished in
the sprint.

There is nobody available
who knows how to
test the one.

Day in Sprint

Figure 1-1 *Mini-waterfall in a sprint*

Finding a High-Value Feature to Start With

Susan and Mark's First Meeting with Jonah

Setting: SUSAN's office.

(SUSAN, MARK, and JONAH are sitting around a table next to a whiteboard.)

MARK: Jonah, let me give you a little background before we dive in. We're looking at creating a system to offer our patrons digital materials like ebooks. Susan has heard from other libraries that nobody likes the off-the-shelf options, so we're considering making our own. But we don't want to spend a bunch of money only to find out our system isn't any better. We'd like to work with you to see if we can get value and feedback earlier and more often in a cost-effective way.

We've been using Scrum for a while, but we still work on big projects with big releases at the end. It seems like we're missing something.

JONAH: OK, there are a few things we can add to Scrum to get you meaningful value and feedback more often. We'll see if we can structure your product backlog to get to "releasable" frequently, and we'll look at something called behavior-driven development, or BDD, to keep your whole team focused on the high-value details and delivering them at a high quality.

Let's start by finding a small, high-value slice of the project you could deliver first. You're testing the hypothesis that you can create a system without the problems of the off-the-shelf alternatives, so let's start with one of those problems.

SUSAN: How about search? I've heard complaints that people can't find the book they want, even if it's actually in the catalog.

JONAH: What do people mostly search by?

MARK: Title, usually. In fact, we know from online search of our print catalog that it's title about 80% of the time.

JONAH: So, could you start with just search by title and see how people use it?

MARK: Yes, and maybe we could give them an opportunity to provide some quick feedback if they don't find what they want in the search results.

SUSAN: Search won't be enough if they can't actually read the book.

MARK: Good point. We have access to a collection of ebooks through Amazon that covers a lot of our most common searches.

JONAH: I'm hearing that you need to include some end-to-end slice of the process from search through borrowing to make this meaningful to users.

SUSAN: That's right.

JONAH: How might we make sure the parts of the process after search don't get too big and delay feedback?

MARK: Well, we could do just a small set of books and only for Kindle. That way, Amazon handles the delivery and expiration of the books.

JONAH: Good. What we're talking about here is what we call a *minimum marketable feature* or MMF. It's the smallest set of functionality that's worth shipping to users, whether you're actually selling it or not. I'm hearing an MMF like, "Find Kindle books by title and borrow them."

(*Writes the MMF title on the whiteboard*)

MARK: That's still pretty big.

JONAH: Sounds like it. Within MMFs, we'll split the work into what we call *user stories*, small slices of system behavior that provide increments of value to users and some visibility into progress for you.

An example story for this MMF might be: "In order to find the specific ebook I'm looking for, as a library patron, I want to search the ebook catalog by title."

MARK: That makes sense.

(JONAH writes the story on the whiteboard)

MARK *(Continues)*: Another one could be, "In order to actually read the book, I want to be able to check out an ebook to my Kindle."

JONAH: Great.

(Writes the story on the whiteboard)

SUSAN: And, "In order to get more ebooks I want in the library, I want to be able to tell a librarian when searching by title that I didn't find the book I wanted."

(JONAH writes the story on the whiteboard)

JONAH: If you delivered those three stories, would it be worth getting in front of real users?

MARK: I think so.

(SUSAN nods)

JONAH: Great. Let's pull in some of the team members to flesh out more details for those stories so they can get started. Mark, can you snap a photo of the board for our next conversation?

MARK: Sure.

(Takes a photo of the whiteboard)

Before You Start with Cucumber

Recall from our definition at the start of this chapter that BDD is about using concrete examples to develop the right software. To come up with good examples and to build features example by example, getting feedback along the way, the work must be organized in slices that deliver value. If you don't have good functional slices—if you're building components or doing technical tasks—you'll end up with scenarios that look more like developer-facing unit tests than like examples of valuable system behavior from a user's perspective.

Finding the First MMF

An MMF is a good place to start. MMF stands for *minimum marketable feature*.[2] It's a small slice (minimum) of new functionality (feature) with enough of an impact to be worth getting in front of real users (marketable).

This is analogous to the concept of a minimum effective dose (MED) in medicine. Consider, for example, acetaminophen, a common drug for pain relief. Taking 5 mg has no effect. For a typical adult, 650 mg can make pain go away for a few hours. But as little as 7500 mg can cause acute liver failure. More isn't better—it's worse. We want to use as little of a drug as we can to achieve the desired impact because drugs have side effects. This amount is the minimum effective dose. Likewise, developing too much of a feature has side effects: delays, missed market windows, opportunity costs, waste, and so on. We want to build the minimum amount of feature to have the desired business impact and no more.

To get at the first MMF or two from a big idea, we recommend a technique we call feature mining:

1. Get a few people in the same room (or virtual equivalent) to represent both the business and the technical perspectives for this project.

2. Together, brainstorm answers on a whiteboard or set of flip charts to these four questions:

    1. Where's the value or impact? (Why is this worth doing? What benefits will go to whom?)

    2. What makes it big? (Why do we need to slice it at all? What is there many or much of? What always takes a long time, even if it's well understood?)

    3. Where are the risks? (What irreversible negative consequences could happen?) Write these as statements of the risk being realized (for example, "We're not able to optimize the performance enough for the reports to run overnight," not just, "Performance").

    4. Where are uncertainties? (What important questions do we need to answer for this to succeed?)

---

2. *Software by Numbers*, Mark Denne and Jane Cleland-Huang, p. 5ff

3. When you get more than one or two answers to a question, identify the most important answers to each question, as shown in Figure 1-2. With a larger group, you might need to use a technique like dot voting to get a quick answer. To dot vote, give each participant three dot stickers per list. They can apply their dots all on one item in the list, or they can spread the dots across two or three items.

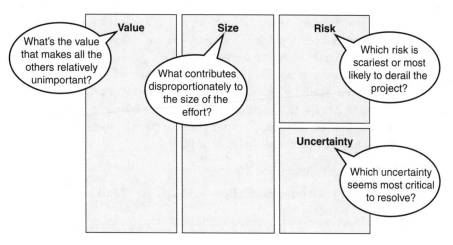

Figure 1-2 *Identifying the most important answer to each feature mining question*

4. Brainstorm possible ways to slice the big idea that get you a good piece of the value, perhaps some risk mitigation and learning, but without all the things that make the project big. We like to ask the following while pointing at the corresponding most important answers in each column:

"How can **we get some of this top impact** without taking on all this 'bigness'? What if we just…"

"How can **we mitigate this risk** without taking on all this 'bigness'? What if we just…"

"How can **we answer this question** without taking on all this 'bigness'? What if we just…"

5. Identify an MFF to start with. It's often the intersection of more than one of your possible ways to slice.

Once you have the first MMF or two, the next MMFs tend to follow pretty naturally. Occasionally, the first MMFs address a major risk or uncertainty, and after completing those, it's necessary to do another round of feature mining with the new information you gained from building the first MMFs.

When we first started using this approach, we were afraid we'd run into projects where the value and what made the project big were inextricably linked. If we wanted to get the value early, we'd have to take on the hard parts first. Surprisingly, as we've done this over and over with different clients, we've found that the biggest contributor to value and the biggest contributor to size rarely intersect. There's usually an 80/20 pattern where a relatively small effort contributes a disproportionately large slice of value. Then, there are diminishing returns as you have to start doing the hard parts to claw out the rest of the value. (Of course, you can always stop with the 80% and move on to the next 80/20 slice of something else.)

After a while, this process becomes more intuitive. Jonah was able to help Susan and Mark find a first MMF by prodding about value, effort, risk, and uncertainty without formally facilitating the meeting described earlier. But when you're first getting started approaching projects in a new way, taking it step by step builds the skills and mindset you need to eventually do this more fluently.

Hallway Conversation Between Jonah and Mark

JONAH: Mark, how was that meeting different from other product planning meetings you've had in the past?

MARK: In the past, any positive conversations with our stakeholders around a product were about them adding scope. To have a conversation about focusing and finding something small and valuable and have it be so collaborative was new for me. We got to agreement so quickly. If this is typical, I'm looking forward to spending less time in contentious meetings.

That MMF is an interesting concept. I like how we're making the work small while still making sure we're delivering enough value to mean something.

I'm still uneasy about not having a plan for the whole system, but I'm willing to run with this for a while and see where it goes.

Slicing an MMF into User Stories

Even if your first MMF is truly *minimal*, it's almost certainly more than a few days of work. It might even be more than a sprint's worth of work. As the Agile Manifesto says, "Working software is the primary measure of progress,"[3] so it would be

---

3. https://agilemanifesto.org/

nice to have real, working slices of new functionality before getting to the end of the MMF. You could organize your work around architectural components and tasks—as many teams do—but these tend to mislead you about your progress and limit your ability to get quality feedback along the way. Instead, we recommend slicing an MMF into user stories.

What's a User Story?

A *user story* is a description of a change in system behavior from the perspective of a user. Each story should add an increment of value, but you will likely have to accumulate a handful of stories before you have enough value to be worth shipping (hence the MMF). Nonetheless, because user stories are complete slices of new behavior, they give a better indicator of progress toward the MMF and a better increment for seeking feedback from stakeholders.

Stories often follow the format: "As a <role> I want <action/feature> so that <value/goal>." Or, sometimes, stories will use an alternative format: "In order to <value/goal>, as a…" The format isn't the important thing, though. What's important is answering the questions raised by the template: Who wants this? What do they want? Why?

To that end, teams who use stories fluently rarely write a story in one of those formats. Instead, they'll answer the three questions in different places. If a story is for the main role, which is described in a product vision, they'll omit the role for that story. They'll use a short, two- to four-word title at the top of the story card or in the story title field in a digital tool. And they'll just write the "why" on the card or in the story description field. It looks something like that shown in Figure 1-3.

So how do you get good user stories from an MMF? Just as you did with feature mining to slice a big idea into MMFs, you can ask the four questions about value, size, risk, and uncertainty. At the MMF level, though, you'll often have enough of an understanding of value, risk, and uncertainty from doing feature mining that you won't need to formally answer those questions. The interesting question here is, "What makes this particular MMF big?"

Patterns for Splitting Features and Big Stories

There are some common patterns for what makes features big and corresponding ways to split through that complexity to get good user stories. Let's look at a few.[4]

Sometimes an MMF is big because it describes a workflow with multiple steps. If you can describe the user experience of your feature with at least three boxes and

---

4. For more on feature and story splitting, visit http://agileforall.com/splitting-user-stories/, where Richard has written extensively on the topic. This section is a condensation of the content there.

with arrows between them, as shown in Figure 1-4, you probably have one of these workflow features.

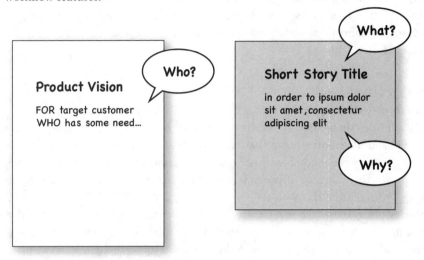

Figure 1-3 *An alternative to the usual user story format*

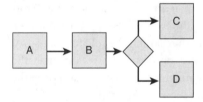

Figure 1-4 *A typical workflow diagram*

In this case, look for a story that takes a thin slice through the whole workflow. For example, if you had a feature about finding and borrowing a book, you might split it so that the first story only offers the opportunity to borrow one hard-coded book, or you might allow patrons to find and borrow a book but not to accumulate multiple books in a cart and borrow them all at once. Then, write additional stories to account for the missing pieces to flesh out that workflow.

Sometimes an MMF is big because it includes multiple operations, where you're allowing the user to manage some entity in the system. In this case, you could split the feature into a story for each of these operations. For example, "Manage my library account" easily splits into

- Create my account
- View my account details

- Change my password
- Change my account details
- Cancel my account
- Etc.

Other times the MMF is big because it includes many business rule variations, which we could split across multiple stories. In Chapter 6, "Making Scenarios More Expressive," we look at an example of the library team working on the logic around fines for returning books late. There are many different business rules for fines based on whether you've borrowed a book or a DVD, for example, or whether you're a child or an adult. These rules can be sliced into separate stories.

Sometimes, it's not the variety of rules that makes a feature big but the variety of data that needs to be tested through those rules. For example, maybe the library catalog needs to support multiple languages. The rules are the same for each language, but working with the different languages may reveal edge cases and bugs, so each significant variation needs to be tested. You might choose to start with just one or two representative languages rather than supporting all of them from the beginning.

Occasionally, a complex user interface makes a feature big. In that case, we can often slice the feature to use a simple interface first and enhance it with the full-featured interface later. This is particularly useful when the value or learning is mostly associated with the behavior rather than the interface, and the interface just adds incremental value.

Often a feature has a simple core, a "happy path," with many variations and enhancements. That simple core can be its own story, and then the variations can be grouped into several more stories. This approach helps you focus on what really matters in a feature. You might not even end up building some of the variations.

Choosing a Story to Start With

So, you've split your MMF into a handful of user stories; which one do you start with? Does it even matter? An MMF, by definition, will be released as a single unit. We've defined anything less than the MMF as less than marketable. So, we don't worry much about prioritizing by value within an MMF. Instead, we prefer to prioritize by learning and risk mitigation. We'll look for a story that will teach us something about the problem or solution. Often, this is the story that will get us the most feedback from a key stakeholder to confirm that we're solving the right problem or solving it in a useful way. We can safely leave the least risky or least informative stories for last.

If you've used feature mining to find your MMF, you probably already listed the questions you need to answer and risks you need to mitigate. These lists can help you prioritize the stories.

Keeping It Minimal

As you split an MMF, you'll think of new variations you weren't aware of at the beginning. Remember the first M of MMF, minimum. Each story should earn its way into the MMF. Ask yourself questions like, "Is this story essential to this MMF or is it something we could come back to later?" You don't want nice-to-have stories holding essential stories hostage.

Summary

- BDD is *exploring desired system behavior with examples in conversations and formalizing examples into automated tests to guide development.*

- BDD is primarily a way of collaborating, not primarily a test automation approach.

- Approaches like Scrum are good, but insufficient, because teams often do mini-waterfalls within or across sprints. BDD can help teams avoid mini-waterfalls.

- A prerequisite to BDD is work organized into slices of value. We recommend minimum marketable features (MMFs) and user stories for this.

- Feature mining can help you find your first MMF from a big idea.

- You can split MMFs into user stories using patterns like thin slices through a workflow, stories for business role variations, stories for different operations, and stories for data variations.

- Start with the story that will teach you something or mitigate a key risk.

- Keep your MMFs minimal by making each story earn its way into the MMF.

- Once you have at least one good MMF with at least one good user story (and a cross-functional team to work on it), you're ready to proceed with BDD.

Reference

Denne, Mark, and Jane Cleland-Huang. *Software by Numbers: Low-Risk, High-Return Development.* Santa Clara, CA: Sun Microsystems, Inc., 2004.

Chapter 2

Exploring with Examples

As we said in Chapter 1, "Focusing on Value," the first and most important part of BDD is exploring desired system behavior with examples in conversations.

We set the stage for conversations around examples by finding valuable slices of functionality on which to focus in the form of MMFs and user stories. In this chapter, we look at how to explore the behavior of a new user story by collaborating around examples with a cross-functional team.

Involving the Team to Describe a Story with Examples

First Whole Team Meeting

ROBIN: A developer. Joined the team a month ago after working for several startups in the Bay Area. She's familiar with Agile and has a voracious appetite for learning the latest tools, techniques, and applications.

RAJ: Senior developer on the team. Has an MSc in Computer Science and has been working in library systems for many years.

JANE: Tester. She has a poster in her cube that says, "A failure to plan on your part does not constitute an emergency on mine." Very focused on her work and enthusiastic about trying things that can help her be more effective and efficient.

JESSIE: ScrumMaster. Started out as a web designer, but after seeing another ScrumMaster in action she realized she might enjoy trying that. Fantastic at digging in and helping the team solve their impediments, often so seamlessly that the team doesn't realize she did it, attributing it to coincidence or themselves. She's OK with that.

SAM: Business analyst. Sam is a late adopter, very pragmatic, structured, and process-oriented. He was attracted to becoming a BA because he likes putting things in order. After a few beers he might tell you he understands the library processes better than the librarians do.

Setting: A small conference room in the library's downtown office. There is a conference table with eight chairs and a pile of sticky notes, and an empty whiteboard along one wall.

(MARK, ROBIN, RAJ, JANE, JONAH, JESSIE, and SAM have assembled in the conference room and are waiting for MARK to start the meeting.)

MARK (*Product Owner*): Hi, everyone. As you all know, we've developed a lot of great software and generally have done a good job of keeping most of our library patrons happy. In our last project retrospective, we said we wanted to get better at communicating about scope and reducing rework. This new project seemed like a good opportunity to experiment with a new way of working together.

I mentioned yesterday that I would be bringing in Jonah to help coach us in some new approaches and techniques to help us collaborate and communicate better. Since you've all just come off a successful release, Susan, Jessie, and I agreed it might be best to treat what we do here as an experiment, as a "proof of concept" for these techniques.

We'll still be developing production-ready software but "kicking the tires" on learning BDD with Cucumber as we do it. So, we've set aside the next week or so to work on our first feature, with coaching help from Jonah along the way. It will be outside our regular sprint approach to give us a little more freedom to experiment and learn. How does that sound to everyone?

(Nods of agreement around the room)

RAJ (*Developer*): Sounds great. This approach gives us a chance to try some things without the regular pressure of deadlines and make mistakes as we learn. Plus, we're still delivering real features.

I've been doing Scrum for so long now, though, it will feel a little weird to not follow the sprint structure.

JESSIE (*ScrumMaster*): Agreed. It's just something Mark and I thought might help you all feel more comfortable as you ramp up. Let's still meet for our regular daily standups, but we'll treat demos as something we do once we feel like we're ready, rather than trying to work to a regular sprint schedule.

MARK (Product Owner): Works for me. Looks like we're all in agreement.

Jonah, you had a conversation with Robin, Raj, and Jane yesterday afternoon about tooling for this, right? I assume we're all on board with using Cucumber to support testing the features as we develop them.

JONAH (Coach): Thanks, Mark. Yes, yesterday I stopped by the team area and Robin, Raj, Jane, and I talked through the change in approach and new tooling that you'll be experimenting with as a team. They've also each watched a BDD overview video online I had pointed out to them.

ROBIN (Developer): I can't wait to try this out! Cucumber looks very cool and I've wanted to play with Capybara for a long time now but not had the chance.

RAJ (Developer): It looks intriguing.

JANE (Tester): I'm really hoping this will mean I won't have to deal with lots of functionality to test at the end of each sprint like the last release, but we'll see. It should at least reduce the amount of manual testing I do and help with regression testing in the future.

MARK (Product Owner): Sam, how about you?

SAM (Business Analyst): I don't know what you're all talking about.

MARK (Product Owner): What?

JONAH (Coach): Sam, I apologize. I tried to loop you into yesterday's conversation, but your office door was shut and it looked like you were meeting with someone at the time. It's unfortunate that you weren't able to be part of the introduction. Are you available after this meeting to talk through any questions you might have?

SAM (Business Analyst): Sure, no problem.

JONAH (Coach): Excellent. I'll also talk you through the same things I went through with the others and send you a link to the same video.

What we're going to practice in this meeting is having a conversation together about a new feature for the library website, talking about what "done" means for that story, and gathering some examples that we'll later turn into test scenarios.

MARK (Product Owner): Help me understand, Jonah. Is what you just described the essentials of the "BDD process" you described to me earlier?

JONAH (Coach): Conversations about the user goals for features, examples of how the business works and how that feature fits into the business processes are an important part of BDD for sure. We'll be using business examples to help us have a shared understanding of software we need to build. There's more to BDD than just those things, though.

One comment I'll make is about BDD being a "process." What comes to mind when you think of "process?"

RAJ (Developer): I think of something heavyweight, like RUP. Something that has a lot of steps and roles and approvals.

MARK (Product Owner): Before we adopted Scrum, our process was really heavyweight: many approvals and lots of waste, and lots of competition over scope between the business and our teams. We tried to keep the scope under control, and the business tried to cram everything they could into the requirements document because they got only one shot at it. But, in terms of Agile, when I think of process I think of Scrum. It has a minimal set of roles, artifacts, and meetings. It can seem like a lot, but it's not really. So process doesn't have to be a bad word.

ROBIN (Developer): Right, me too. I think of overhead, and having to do things just because the process says so, even when it doesn't make sense. One thing I liked about doing Agile in the startups I used to work for is there was minimal process overhead compared with the first job I had out of college.

JONAH (Coach): What about a game? What comes to mind when I say the word "game?"

JANE (Tester): Something like basketball, I suppose. A team of people working together, playing positions, helping each other, trying to win against the other team.

SAM (Business Analyst): A game has a goal, like winning against the other team. And you need skilled players used to playing together to achieve the goal. The players have to adjust their strategy on the fly as the game progresses.

ROBIN (Developer): A game should be fun.

JONAH (Coach): You've got it. Why do I ask this? Mainly because I view BDD much more like a game than a process. BDD has a goal, it takes a team working together, team members need to grow their skills over time with individual and team practice, and the team positions and strategy are fluid as the game progresses. And BDD, like any game worth playing, can be very challenging and demanding, but the rewards are worth it. As the team improves over time, playing the BDD game should be fun and fulfilling.

SAM (Business Analyst): But games are trivial things; they are for children. We should be software professionals, not "software hedonists."

JONAH (Coach): Right. The goal isn't the fun, that's a good side effect, though I do believe people who enjoy their work are much more likely to be productive than those who don't. Don't mistake the word "game" for something trivial or just for children, though. Games are invented and used by many people, including novelists, military tacticians, mathematicians, game theorists, and corporate strategists.

So, think of BDD more like a game than a process as we move forward. Like any game, it takes a bit of practice to learn it. And you shouldn't expect to be good at it right away, especially since it involves discerning goals and learning to work more closely together as a team to achieve those goals.

Let me say again, in this meeting we'll be trying an approach that is going to feel new and different, maybe even weird and counterintuitive, to most of you at first, so I'd encourage you to roll with it and see where it takes us. Have fun with it. If any of you have concerns or questions then feel free to grab me later and I'll do my best to address them.

BDD Is a Cooperative Game

In Alistair Cockburn's book *Agile Software Development: The Cooperative Game*, he characterizes software development as a "cooperative game of invention and communication." In competitive games, like tennis, there is a clear notion of winning and losing. Even in team games, like basketball, one team wins and the other loses. But in cooperative games, people work to win together.

Games can also be finite or infinite. A finite game, like chess, is one that intends to have an end. On the other hand, an infinite game, like the game an organization or nation typically plays, is about prolonging one's existence.

Games can be finite and goal-seeking, like chess, or they can be finite and non-goal-directed, like jazz, where the process is the focus—there's not a defined goal that would cause you to "win" the song.

If we combine these ideas to get a goal-seeking, finite, cooperative game, we see activities like rock climbing or adventure racing, where a group of people work together to reach a goal together as fast as possible. Software development, especially Agile software development, is a similar game. *Software development is a finite, goal-seeking, cooperative, group game.*

BDD is an Agile subdiscipline of the game of software development. The emphasis in BDD is particularly placed on helping the team cooperate, innovate, and communicate during the game, all with the intention of achieving the goal of creating valuable working software more quickly and effectively.

BDD Is a Whole Team Thing

Teams who find their way into BDD via a tool like Cucumber often get the misunderstanding that BDD is a test automation approach that mostly concerns testers and developers.

BDD is a whole-team practice. It's a way of structuring the collaboration required to build the right software. As such, it involves all the roles on the team.

Product owners bring an understanding of the customer and realistic examples of a user doing something with the software. Testers bring their unique perspectives about what could go wrong; they're great at proposing examples outside the happy path. Developers understand the implications of a particular example on implementation and often have a good understanding of the existing system and the problems it solves. Technical writers contribute skills with language and often empathy for how users talk about what they do in the system.

Early in adopting BDD, collaboration tends to occur as a whole team. This allows the team to build a common language for their domain. Later, smaller groups can leverage that language to collaborate, and the work they produce will be comprehensible to the rest of the team.

Because we see so much value in the whole team participating in the collaboration in BDD, we rarely teach public BDD classes. If only some team members understand how to work in this way, the team is unlikely to experience the benefits. We've seen cases where just the testers or just the developers get excited about a tool like Cucumber and just end up doing test automation, the least valuable part of BDD, in isolation.

Allow Time and Space to Learn

Did you notice how Jonah warned the team it wasn't going to be easy? Adopting a new way of working takes time and practice. It takes a willingness to muddle through until the new skills become natural. It's easy to forget what we went through to adopt our current skills—they weren't always as natural as they seem now.

Sometimes it feels like you can't afford the time to learn something new. Maybe someone committed you to deliver a big project (with defined scope) by a particular date, and it doesn't feel like you have any room to slow down. In that case, feature mining from Chapter 1 is your secret weapon.

These big release or project commitments that feel so fixed and overwhelming are usually fairly high-level. We know we have to deliver, say, the new sales reporting by June 15. But within the bullet point of "new sales reporting," there's high-value work and there's low-value work. Feature mining gives us a way to focus on the high-value work and avoid the low-value work, thereby making the deadline less scary and buying some extra capacity for improvement.

We also don't recommend adopting a new practice like BDD for all your work all at once. Instead, we recommend you use what we call the "slow lane" approach. Say you've planned eight user stories in your sprint. Most stories will use your existing definition of done, which doesn't include BDD. Choose one or two to be in the "slow lane" across your board (see Figure 2-1). For those, you'll use the new practice. And you won't feel as pressured when you do it because you've already agreed those will take longer.

The early adopters on your team who are excited about the new practice will tend to sign up for those stories, working out the issues and establishing patterns for those who prefer to "wait and see."

After a while, expand the slow lane to three or four stories. Eventually, you'll notice that the stories with the new practice really aren't that much slower (and probably turn out faster in the end because they have fewer defects and less rework). At that point, make the new practice part of your definition of done for every story.

Some teams move from the slow lane to fully adopting BDD in just two or three sprints. Others take their time and do it over four to six months. There's no rush. It's better to adopt a practice slowly, deliberately, and well than to rush into it badly and give up under pressure.

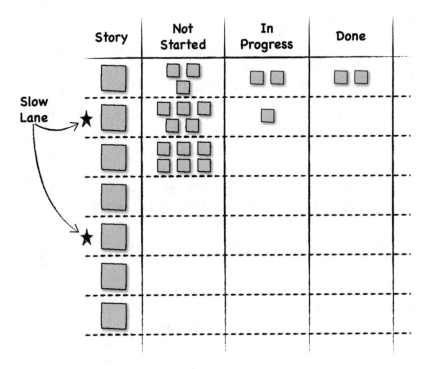

Figure 2-1 *A task board with two stories designated as slow lane stories*

The Meeting Continues…

JONAH: Mark, how about you start by introducing the feature you'll be developing first?

MARK: Sure. Thanks, Jonah.

Well, the first minimal marketable feature, or MMF, is about borrowing an ebook from Amazon. Our first story is implementing searching for an ebook.

JONAH: Let's use sticky notes to put some structure around our discussion. Mark, use one of these yellow rectangle stickies to capture the story at the top of the whiteboard.

MARK: *(Writes on sticky note)* In order to find the specific ebook I'm looking for, as a library patron, I want to search the ebook catalog by title. *(Sticks it to the whiteboard)*

ROBIN: We've been using user stories in our backlog, but they're a little different in form from this one. I like how you put the "In order…" first to highlight the value to the library patron as a customer-facing feature. This is nice.

JONAH: Good observation, Robin. That format is all about focusing on "why" rather than just "what." I'd encourage you all not to focus too much on the format, though. A user story should function as a reminder to have a conversation about the user need being met.

Mark, why don't you give a little background on why we are going to focus on this story in particular?

MARK: Sure. We've seen that people search on title about 80% of the time. So, they know which book they want to find. Currently, the catalog search returns too many unrelated titles in its results, and even when the correct title is returned near the top of the results, it takes too long, and the results are presented in a way that's confusing to our patrons. It's no surprise we've had complaints from library patrons about not being able to find books we actually have in the catalog.

What we want to do is dip our toes in the waters of digital materials but do it with a minimum investment in custom software development. We want to offer a small set of ebooks and only for Kindle. That way, Amazon will take care of the delivery and expiration of the books and we don't need to worry about that. So, Susan and I agreed we could start by building out a new search by title for Kindle ebooks to see how our patrons use it.

JONAH: I wanted to let you know that Raj, Mark, and I talked yesterday and instead of rewriting your legacy system, you'll be adding these new capabilities over the top of the existing system. Taking this approach will dramatically reduce your risk while enabling you to get the new work done quickly, since you won't be bogged down in trying to improve code that's not associated with new value you're adding.

RAJ: Yes, after talking with Mark earlier about this MMF I had expected to spend a couple of weeks sketching out the architecture for a complete ebook management system or figuring out how to rewrite the current catalog module in our legacy integrated library system.

I've wanted to rewrite our legacy ILS for years, but I always suspected we'd never finish it and would soon find ourselves with *two* legacy ILSs to support.

JONAH: *(Laughs)* Yes, that's the typical outcome of that approach. Avoid it wherever possible. Better to take a more strategic approach to replacing capabilities within an older system.

RAJ: Instead of rewriting, we're going pull the Kindle ebook metadata directly from Amazon and use it to enrich our existing catalog in our ILS, rather than try to track the digital inventory separately from our current ILS catalog inventory. So, the first thing is to augment our legacy system rather than try to rewrite it. That will save us a lot of time and minimize our risk, especially when we are trying to learn BDD as well.

JONAH: A second approach you're taking that will help a lot is to leverage open source for the generic parts of your system—right, Raj?

RAJ: Yes, absolutely. I've found a great open-source library to use for search. The catalog team has already configured the backend system to exclude ebooks from regular searches. Jonah and I sketched it all out on the whiteboard in the team area if anyone's interested.

JONAH: Raj was able to come up with a really elegant and clean way of integrating this open-source search framework with your current ILS, avoiding having to write your own search code or try to rewrite any of your ILS. Double win!

ROBIN: That's great news.

JONAH: Let's capture assumptions and questions on pink stickies next to the story to keep us focused. I've heard three key assumptions so far. *(Writes on stickies as he talks)*

Using Amazon Kindle ebook metadata

Adding to the current ILS

Using OS search framework

(Sticks them to whiteboard next to the story card)

ROBIN: OK, dumb question time. I'm looking at the story and, as you know, I'm pretty new on the team and haven't done development work for a library before, so I want to be clear on what you mean by "title."

Are you talking about the *name* of a book or what comes back in the search results, or is it something else? And how does this work with ebooks? Are you meaning Kindle, epub, mobi, audiobooks, mp3...or are there other formats?

MARK: No, those are fundamental library concepts we all need to understand. There's no dumb question there.

JONAH: Robin is asking some great questions about the library domain. I suggest that rather than ask for definitions, let's focus on specific examples. For example, let's pretend Robin asked, "I don't really know what you mean by *title*—can you give me a typical *example* of an ebook title?"

SAM: Well, there are actually some nuances about *title* that we don't really need to worry about now. Mark, I suggest for now we just use *title* to be the name of the book, and we can come back later and talk about the other ways *title* gets used around here.

ROBIN: No problem.

JANE: Actually, Jonah's suggestion about using examples is a good one. It would help us all get on the same page about how the search needs to work. I'm typically working off specific examples in my current test plans.

JONAH: Right. To build on that a little: Since we are talking about Kindle ebooks... Mark, for starters, can you give us an example of an ebook that one of our library patrons would actually be searching for?

MARK: OK. Sure, hmmm. What's a good example? Let's say fantasy fiction author Brandon Sanderson releases a new title in his *Stormlight Archive* series and it gets released on Kindle. Each of these has been a bestseller in the past, so we know any new book in the series is going to be in very high demand. For example, *Words of Radiance* debuted at #1 on the *New York Times* Hardcover Fiction Bestseller list in early 2014, and the ebook reached #1 on the combined print/ebook bestseller list. So, how about we use *Words of Radiance* as our example?

ROBIN: Good choice! I've been enjoying that series.

(*JANE picks up a marker to write the example. JONAH hands Jane a pad of green sticky notes.*)

JANE: *(Writes "Find an ebook by the exact title: Words of Radiance" and sticks it on the whiteboard.)*

I'm not much of a fantasy reader, but *(Looking meaningfully in Robin's direction)* I have friends who are. Sounds like a good one to start with. Let me capture this on the whiteboard.

(Writing on a pink sticky note) I'll also capture Robin's earlier question about titles, so we can get that up on the whiteboard for later too.

SAM: So, we're assuming we already have *Words of Radiance* in the catalog, right? Cause if we don't, then the search results would be different.

MARK: Well, we need to handle the situation where it doesn't show up in the search results. That's part of assumptions for this story.

JONAH: Sam and Mark both have a good point, I'd encourage you to stick with the simple case for now—the "happy path"—so we can dig into its nuances. We can capture any other scenarios and come back to them later.

Let's capture the rule for the happy path. I'll call it "Matches title word for word" and put that above the example on the board. *(Writes on a blue sticky note)*

This makes me want the counter example. I'll call it "Doesn't find the book: *Words Radiance*". *(Writes on a green sticky note)*

JANE: I just noticed something: Since *Words of Radiance* will be in the catalog, this choice of example means we won't have to do test data setup and teardown for this story. We can simply test against the real catalog because the Amazon Kindle ebook metadata will have been loaded into it.

JONAH: It's a nice outcome from taking Raj's approach. It's not a long-term approach, of course—we're going to need to figure out how to get the catalog into a particular state for scenarios later—but it will help you get up and running quickly without getting bogged down in technical issues.

At this point, you have complexity in a lot of areas: you're building a whole new set of capabilities for your customers, solving new technical problems, and exploring a new way of working together. Deferring technical complexity for now is a nice way to get to customer value faster. However, we'll want to set up a time soon to talk about how you'll handle the data setup problem when you get there.

> *RAJ*: Yes, it's a big relief. I was worried about how we would handle the whole test data side of things.
>
> *JONAH*: Exactly. Let's not bite off too much infrastructure stuff at this point. We'll deal with it soon enough.
>
> *JESSIE*: OK, I'll capture that "missing title" scenario for later reference then. *(Writes "Search for an ebook by exact title but missing from our catalog" on a sticky note and puts it on the whiteboard)*

Flesh Out the Happy Path First

It's often easy to come up with a bunch of examples right away, but we recommend talking all the way through at least one core example before getting deep in variations. By talking through a "happy path" example, a common case where things work as they should, the team gets a shared understanding of what the user story is about. What does it look like when the user is able to do what they want to do?

This complete slice also helps validate the story. Sometimes a story that sounds quite reasonable in the abstract reveals mistaken assumptions when you get into a core example. "Wait a minute," someone says, "no user would actually do it that way."

Once everyone understands the happy path, it often becomes more clear which variations are reasonable and likely. Instead of brainstorming every possible variation and edge case, realistic examples float to the top and focus the team on getting to value quickly. (The less likely variations and edge cases can be useful for exploratory testing, by the way. More on this and how it relates to BDD in Chapter 3, "Formalizing Examples into Scenarios.")

Use Real Examples

Notice the team's happy path example wasn't just about "a book" or "Title ASDF"; it was an example of a real book that a real library patron might borrow. Good examples put you in the user's shoes, building empathy for what the user is trying to do and helping you think more accurately about how they'll do it.

It wasn't a coincidence that using *Words of Radiance* for the example led the team to realize they already had test data to use. A real example connected the team to the system full of real inventory they already had at the library. This is not unusual. One real thing connects to other real things. We frequently see teams make discoveries about functionality, design, and architecture when they get into concrete, realistic examples.

Example Mapping Gives the Discussion Structure

Our favorite way to add some light structure to this kind of discussion is with Matt Wynne's Example Mapping technique.[1] In Example Mapping, the group builds a tree: the story has rules that are illustrated by examples. Assumptions and questions are captured on the side so the core discussion about examples doesn't get blocked by side conversations. The result looks something like Figure 2-2.

Discussions about examples necessarily lead to rabbit trails—side topics that could distract from the core topic—because reality is complex and interlinked. In the meeting we just looked at, the team allowed side topics to naturally emerge but retained focus on the core topic with a facilitation tool called a parking lot. The parking lot is simply a place to capture things that are worth talking about but not right now.

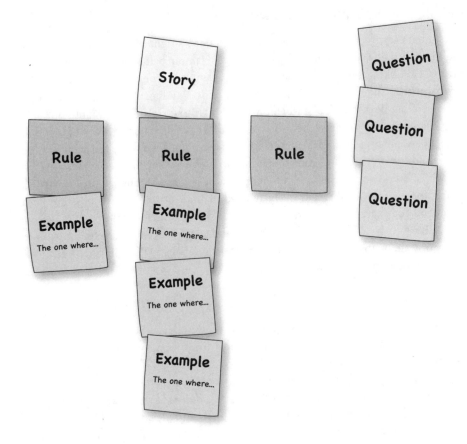

Figure 2-2 *Example Mapping*

---

1. https://docs.cucumber.io/bdd/example-mapping/

In Example Mapping, pink stickies typically function as the parking lot—the questions and assumptions that otherwise might take over the discussion. But yellow, green, or blue stickies could capture stories, examples, or rules to be included in a future discussion.

Jane captured a note about audiobooks, for example. Audiobooks were explicitly out of scope for the current feature, but they were worth thinking about. Mark will probably take that note, convert it into a product backlog item, and prioritize it appropriately.

Using a parking lot balances the needs to be open to diverse contributions and to capture important discussion topics with the need to respect meeting participants' time by keeping the meeting focused. We use variations on this technique in almost everything we facilitate.

Back to the Meeting…

RAJ: Back to Robin's question again, there are multiple formats we support, so we might have *Words of Radiance* in mobi for the Kindle and epub for Apple, and as an audiobook in mp3.

ROBIN: That's what I thought: The first two are alternatives to getting the hardcover or paperback book, for people looking for electronic reading formats, whereas mp3 is for people who would rather listen to the book.

MARK: You're right that there are multiple formats, but that's not a concern for us with this story. As I mentioned before, Susan and I agreed to focus just on Kindle ebooks for now, so let's keep the reading aspect primary and only worry about Kindle format for now.

(JANE writes "no audiobooks for now" on a pink sticky and sticks it to the whiteboard.)

RAJ: I've done a lot with search in the past, and there are many ways to search our catalog: keyword, author, title, and so on. Are we talking about a keyword search here?

MARK: I actually talked about this earlier with Susan, and when we looked at the traditional searches over 80% of them were by title, and the patron picked the book with the matching title.

JESSIE: *(Writing on a sticky note)* Got it, search by title only.

OK, some user experience kinds of questions here: We are assuming the library patron is on our catalog page, correct?

MARK: Yes, catalog page.

JESSIE: OK, good. Also, I'd like us to talk a little about what we can assume or expect about the patron's typical background, goals, and pain points.

JONAH: That's where I was hoping we would head too. What Jessie is concerned about is moving beyond an impersonal notion of the "role" of the system user to something a bit more human, a "persona."

SAM: What do you mean, persona? Isn't this just a story that says something like, "As a library patron, I want to search the library catalog for an ebook"?

JESSIE: True. Jonah and I talked yesterday about starting to incorporate personas into how we do our user experience work. Basically, a persona is a short description of the important characteristics of a certain kind of user—their goals, background, experience, and pain points. Putting together personas will really help us do a better job of user experience going forward, rather than our UI treating all of our users as if they are the same, which they're not. Using personas encourages us to think more from a customer perspective and avoid implementing features our customers won't really need.

JONAH: Right, as a friend of mine says, "A persona's biggest benefit is not to tell us what to include, but to tell us what *not* to."

Yes, Sam, the story will probably look something very similar to that in the product backlog. A story is a placeholder for a team conversation, so I suggest we take a moment to dig a little deeper and put more of a face to whom we mean by *library patron* for this feature.

Mark, can you give us a little background on the library patron you would like this MMF to target?

MARK: Sure. Most of our search users are familiar with Google search and using websites but not much beyond that. They are used to being able to easily find the book they want on Amazon. We would much rather they come to our library than go somewhere else, and so would they.

You mentioned their goal, and I guess it's to find the book they want with as little hassle, and encountering as little confusing technical jargon, as possible. And we decided in that previous meeting that we would only target Kindle users for this story, as Kindle is the most popular platform.

JESSIE: (*Sketching notes about persona on whiteboard*) So we can assume some basic technical background for our typical library patron, but not much. And we want to avoid confusing technical or library-specific jargon in the UI where possible. Are most of them coming through a web browser?

MARK: Yes, correct on all counts. Overly technical jargon in search is a current pain point for many of our users.

ROBIN: So when the user, I mean *library patron*, sees the search results, there will be other books listed, but *Words of Radiance* should be at the top? *Words of Radiance* won't be the only result, right?

MARK *and* SAM: Right.

JONAH: OK, good. So we can make it simple because this first search scenario should talk about having *Words of Radiance* at the top of the search results, but it doesn't need to say anything about what the rest of the search results might be.

MARK: Makes sense to me.

JONAH: It seems like we probably have a good enough shared understanding of the happy path scenarios to stop here. We don't need everyone involved to start formalizing them up a bit for the Cucumber feature file; a few of us can tackle that later.

It would be helpful to take a photo of the whiteboard to capture what we've done so far and send it around. Raj and Robin, would you like me to help you take an initial pass at writing up the scenarios as a feature file?

RAJ: Sure. Jonah, how about you, Robin, and I try doing that right after lunch and we all meet back here to review what we come up with? What do you all think? 3 p.m. work for everyone? Good.

I'll take care of taking the photo of the whiteboard and sending it around too.

MARK: Sounds great. I'll send everyone another meeting invite for this room at 3 p.m. This approach is pretty new to me, so I'm looking forward to seeing what you come up with.

Optimizing for Discovery

You might be surprised that the team proceeds with work on this user story before nailing down all the rules and examples. Rather than working in a series of phases—planning, analysis, development, testing—the team is working iteratively in very small cycles. They're planning and analyzing a little, doing some test design, developing some production code, doing a little more testing, going back to planning, and so on.

The traditional approach to software development assumes we not only have a clear understanding of the goal of a software system but also the means to achieve that goal, and that we know both well ahead of when the software needs to be delivered to the customer. This implies that there is no need to further explore the customer's space, since we already know what the customer requires. The waterfall development process is the logical outcome of this kind of thinking: the means of accomplishing the goal are called *requirements*, and all that is needed is for us to implement the requirements as software features. In industrial work, we want to manage for consistent, repeatable, predictable results; we want our goals to be as clear and unambiguous as possible. Waterfall development takes the same approach as industrial work.

In knowledge work we need to manage for creativity. We are generating something *new* rather than just incrementally improving on the past. This means there is no way to precisely define the goal in advance, because there are too many unknowns. Software development is knowledge work, and Agile development is fundamentally a considered response to this situation of not knowing the exact goal and how to reach it. Agile promotes embracing and adapting to change to be the chief concern of the development process. Thus, teams doing Agile development *optimize for discovery*, as the Manifesto for Agile Software Development says, valuing "responding to change over following a plan." Furthermore, "Agile processes harness change for the customer's competitive advantage."

This ability to respond quickly to new learning is thus at the heart of agility in software development. "The path to the goal is not clear, and the goal may in fact change."[2] An Agile team will often start out with the intention of solving a customer's problem in a certain way but discover their assumptions about that customer need are wrong. They might discover that the real need is actually different from what they thought, which then leads to a very different solution.

There is no such thing as "requirements"; there are only unvalidated assumptions. The goal of delivering MMFs is to validate our assumptions as soon as possible, in case they turn out to be false and we need to change direction. Agile development assumes that the specific destination is unknown, so we need to iterate our way there. Software development is inherently a discovery process.

---

2. *Gamestorming*, p. 5

In knowledge work we need to imagine a world that doesn't exist yet and embrace exploration, experimentation, and trial and error. We are bringing fuzzy goals into reality. A fuzzy goal is one that "motivates the general direction of the work, without blinding the team to opportunities along the journey."[3] This is the journey we hope to demonstrate in this book, as the library development team adopts BDD and employs it to enable them to get better at delivering predictably in the face of fuzzy goals. "Fuzzy goals must give a team a sense of direction and purpose while leaving team members free to follow their intuition."[4]

Addressing Some Concerns

Sam and Jonah Discuss Sam's Concerns

Setting: Sam's office, right after the previous meeting. There are large, colorful, highly detailed business process diagrams plastered over the walls, a couple of comfy chairs, and the scent of fresh coffee.

JONAH: So after I ground the coffee I put it in the Aeropress and made my espresso. And the guy in the seat next to me said, "What on earth is that? Some kind of crazy airpump?"

SAM: *(Laughs)* Seriously? You made your own coffee? Right on the flight here?

JONAH: *(Laughs)* Sounds a little extreme, I know. I usually take the Aeropress when I travel, but that's actually the first time I've used it and the grinder on a plane. I'll probably try it on Friday's flight home—life's too short for in-flight service coffee. Plus it made the cabin smell so much better!

SAM: Ha! No question.

JONAH: Mmmm…This is great coffee, by the way. What is it?

---

3. *Gamestorming*, p. 5
4. *Gamestorming*, p. 5

SAM: Huehuetenango.

JONAH: "Way Way Tenango"? What is that, Ethiopian?

SAM: No, Guatemalan. It's spelled differently from how it sounds. My wife and I vacationed down there last summer and happened to tour through the area where it's grown. Guatemala was an amazing experience, I'll tell you more some other day.

Our day in the village was the highlight, though. We learned so much about the whole coffee process by talking with the people who actually grow it. We've been huge fans of Huehuetenango ever since. It tastes so good, and always brings back those same good memories.

JONAH: I bet. I'll be sure to track down some of my own. Thanks for the tip!

SAM: You're welcome. Anyway, about that last meeting…I might have come off a little strong in there. I don't want you to get the wrong idea, I'm actually very supportive of anything that can help us improve. I just don't like coming into a meeting as the only one not knowing what's going on.

JONAH: No worries. I figured that was the case. Once again, that was not my intention. I'll do everything I can to help get you up to speed.

SAM: Great. As a BA, I tend to work with all the development teams, and sometimes it can be a little hard to keep up with every new thing they're trying. We've had some good success with Scrum recently, but we've also had a lot of tools and initiatives die on the vine. It's hard to know ahead of time what's going to work and what's not. I'm very pragmatic, so I tend to adopt a wait-and-see posture with new things, to see if they deliver on the promise.

As you can see (Gestures around) I'm very process-oriented and always want to keep the bigger picture in mind, so I'm curious as to how this BDD stuff will fit into how the teams work. If this can help bring more structure and discipline to our process, I'm all in favor of it. Will it do that?

JONAH: I expect so. I'd be very surprised if it didn't.

SAM: So, I have some questions. First, what's a feature file?

JONAH: It's what we use to record our test scenarios.

SAM: What? Now I'm confused again. I thought you, Raj, and Robin were going to be writing up the scenarios we captured in this morning's meeting; didn't you say you would be "formalizing them" or something like that?

JONAH: I see. Let me try to clear up some confusion here. Yes, after lunch Raj and Robin and I will do some work formalizing the scenarios we came up with this morning. We'll write them up in what we call a "feature file," which is simply a plain-text description of how we expect the feature to work.

We want to do this formalization to clear up any ambiguities in our language, make sure we captured all the important details, and help us ensure we're all on the same page with you, Mark, and Jane about how it should work. The whole team, actually. It also lets us see if we missed anything.

SAM: Is this where Raj's vegetable makes an appearance? The "cucumber?"

JONAH: Correct! Though cucumbers, like tomatoes, are actually fruit. But that's not important right now.

Anyway, I got us a little off track there. Let's try that again.

There's a software tool called Cucumber that Raj, Robin, and Jane will use in development to treat our scenarios as a kind of "living specification" for the search feature. With Cucumber we'll be able to verify the search feature as they write it. In other words, Raj and Robin will code to the scenarios we create, one by one, running them as tests as they do. The feature file is what Cucumber uses as the place to record the scenarios we are using to specify what the feature should do for this story.

SAM: So this "feature file" is a specification document? We're all in a room just writing a specification document? This is insane. I could do this by myself. We don't need a meeting with the whole team.

Why do we need any meetings for this? Isn't this the kind of thing I would normally do on my own as a business analyst? Actually, on Jessie's team, doesn't someone write all these details in the product backlog item anyway?

JONAH: Good questions. The last thing we want to do is take up everyone's valuable time with useless meetings. We are having more meetings than usual at the moment, since we're getting everyone on the same page with the new techniques, but don't think of BDD as a series of meetings. It's more like something a team just does in the course of development. In other words, in the course of the team doing their work, they collaborate; the right people get together whenever they see the need to figure out details.

SAM: OK, good. I have to admit, the meeting we had earlier today was not like many of the boring meetings we have. Everyone was pretty engaged, and I thought we had some pretty important insights and caught some important cases. I could see how it would be helpful to have the developers and testers as part of that conversation.

JONAH: Exactly. And as you'd expect, I'd love to see you all get to the point where you wouldn't even refer to this sort of thing as "having a meeting," since with BDD if you're describing it as a "meeting" it's usually an indication that something's wrong with your collaboration.

The goal for this morning's conversation was to get the right people in the room to discuss what the story meant and how we'll know it's done, and to make sure we don't miss any important details. It's also critical with a complex business domain like this to ensure the product owner, BAs, developers, and testers—the whole team—are all on the same page with the terminology, how the feature should work, and how it fits in with the rest of the application.

SAM: Yes, there is a lot of complexity in the library domain. More than people appreciate. And all the systems, applications, and integrations we have add a lot of technical complexity too. It's especially hard to build things on top of our legacy ILS.

JONAH: Ah, OK. So, yeah, I would expect that it's hard to build new features on your legacy ILS. Most of the teams I work with are doing BDD over the top of some kind of legacy system. It's a challenge, but it's not a unique one. Or, as I tell people, "Yes, you are a special snowflake, but not in this area."

SAM: (Laughs)

JONAH: Jessie's background in UXD is also very helpful in understanding the flow of user actions and moving beyond just thinking about the role without considering the person using the software and the actual needs the new software feature is intended to meet. I really value having someone who can bring that perspective to the table.

So yes, a feature file is a kind of specification documentation. More like an executable specification. At least, that's what we're aiming for.

SAM: I'm not sure what you mean by "executable specification."

JONAH: In a traditional kind of approach often a product owner, or business analyst such as yourself, would be documenting these scenarios as acceptance criteria, and a tester would perhaps be using them as the basis for their test plan. The acceptance criteria would be captured in the product backlog as stories and their details, and then the test plans and other information would likely be separate supporting documents.

SAM: That's pretty much how we do it now.

JONAH: Right, and much of that part of the process will not change. However, as you can see, feature files are more dynamic than that. They're meant to be *more* than just a document.

With BDD we're aiming for a *living* document, one that grows and changes as the software matures.

Because the scenarios run as tests, they end up automating much of what would normally be recorded in manual test plans and regression tests, and because the developers code *to* the scenarios with Jane's early input, there is less chance of missing things and introducing bugs.

SAM: OK, but won't the feature file have to be constantly changing, such as when we update the UI?

JONAH: If we put a lot of UI-specific language in the feature file, then yes, it certainly would. Many teams fall into that trap by referring to "Submit buttons" and the like. But we won't. We'll take the time to keep only business language in the feature file. That's one area where your input will be invaluable. Help keep us honest!

Teams who do a good job at keeping the feature file language focused on business concerns find the scenarios remain much the same over time. The application's UI may change, and the underlying libraries and applications may too, but the Cucumber scenarios would change only when the actual features change, since they describe the *behavior* of the application in business language, not the implementation. That's a lot to think about. Hopefully, I'm not jumping ahead too much.

SAM: A little. But I'm actually more concerned about where I fit in.

JONAH: Of course. Let's talk about the more important concern, which is *your* role in this kind of approach.

Let's see. Mark understands the big goals, your business goals. But he depends on your understanding of the nuances of business processes, systems, and your domain—all the stuff you're really good at—which is all the stuff that helps the team make sure we have all the right examples for each feature.

SAM: Yes, he does. Mark realizes that no one knows the business processes, technical ecosystem, and even all the library acronyms better than I do. In fact, Mark and Susan kid that after a few beers I might say I understand the library processes better than the librarians do. *(Grins)* But even I wouldn't go that far.

JONAH: (Laughs) In terms of what we're doing this week, this first meeting focused on the happy path, which wasn't really the part where you add the most value. But the next few conversations are where we've got the happy path down, and we'll be going through all the interesting variations. These will be where you're really going to contribute a lot more to this, since it's the part that's really going to depend on you and what you know.

SAM: This first story seems relatively straightforward to me, which is why I'm having some trouble understanding why we're taking so much time on it. At least, it's simple compared to what we'll have to do for tracking what ebooks each library patron is borrowing.

JONAH: Agreed. This first story is less involved when compared to what is coming. Part of that is deliberate, to help your team get up and running with BDD. To start practicing the skills with a simpler example so it's achievable. We'll move to more involved ones once you all have the basic skills down.

SAM: That makes sense. Sometimes I'm the one writing the stories, and sometimes Mark does that. Jessie pitches in, too, from time to time.

Will Mark and I be writing the feature files from now on, or will Raj and Robin do that?

JONAH: There's nothing that says a certain role has to be the one that ends up documenting the scenarios. It's an important process question, so I recommend we hold off on some questions like that for now and see what the team figures out.

Like learning any new team skill, a lot of this is going to be harder to explain ahead of time than just to learn it together by doing it. I'll do my best to answer any questions that come up, and I do really understand how you may be skeptical about trying this approach. I certainly would be if I was in your place. Since you trust the team, I'm sure you can also talk with any of them if you have more concerns.

Why not give it a go, at least for the next few sprints, and see how it works out?

SAM: (Shrugs and nods) OK. I'm willing to give it a try for now, support it, and see what happens.

JONAH: Excellent. Thanks again for the brew! See you after lunch.

Treat Resistance as a Resource

If you're reading this book, you're likely to be an advocate for BDD on your team, which means you're likely to run into resistance from other people who aren't as excited about the change.

You might see that resistance as something you need to fight against to successfully adopt BDD on your team. Or you might write it off as just "resistance to change." We'd like to suggest an alternative: Gratefully accept that resistance as a useful resource.[5]

For the most part, people don't actually resist change per se. People make changes all the time—and that person you think of as "resistant to change" would eagerly change many things in their life if they were to win the lottery. But people do resist particular changes, changes where they don't, for whatever reason, see a likely net positive outcome. This means that when you encounter resistance, you have an opportunity to learn something that might improve your proposed change. When

---

5. Emery, "Resistance as a Resource"

someone resists your proposed change, ask yourself, "What do they know that I don't know?"

To answer that question, we've found it useful to think in terms of different layers of resistance, or layers of buy-in, based on a model from Eli Goldratt's Theory of Constraints. There are several different formulations of this, with different numbers of layers, but we like Dr. K. J. Youngman's:

1. We don't agree about the extent or nature of the problem.

2. We don't agree about the direction or completeness of the solution.

3. We can see additional negative outcomes.

4. We can see real obstacles.

5. We doubt the collaboration of others.[6]

Start at the beginning of the list and look for where the resistance begins. Maybe the person agrees there's a problem to solve but they're not convinced your proposal actually solves it. Find out what they know about the solution; perhaps they've seen something similar in the past that didn't work. You might be able to learn something from that failure. Or, you might be able to persuade them that this solution is different.

Maybe they agree the solution will work but they also see potential side effects. Again, what do they know that you don't? Perhaps you need to add something to your proposed change to mitigate the side effects.

In the previous conversation, Jonah engaged Sam to explore Sam's resistance. Sam had three main objections, all at level 3:

- BDD will cause us to spend too much time in meetings.

- Feature files will have to change too often.

- My role will be marginalized or unappreciated in this new approach.

Notice that Sam wasn't objecting that things were fine and there was no need to change (level 1) or that BDD wouldn't solve their problems (level 2). He was saying that, even if it worked, BDD would cause negative side effects. So, Jonah engaged Sam in conversation about those potential side effects and how to prevent or mitigate them. Had Jonah focused on the problem and how BDD would solve it, he wouldn't have

---

6. Youngman, http://www.dbrmfg.co.nz/Bottom%20Line%20Agreement%20to%20Change.htm

won Sam's willingness to participate in the experiment. Sam might even have worked against the experiment. But because Jonah heard and engaged Sam's concerns, Sam's on board and his feedback can help make the experiment stronger.

One pleasant surprise with this approach to resistance is how often the person putting up the biggest resistance becomes the biggest supporter of the change once you listen to them and incorporate what they know.

Playing the BDD Game

Jonah introduced the idea that BDD, like Agile, is a cooperative game. Let's dig in to some of the practical implications of this as we think about exploring examples. The book *Gamestorming* presents the idea that every game has a common shape. This shape has three different stages, and each stage has a different purpose. This shape looks like that shown in Figure 2-3.

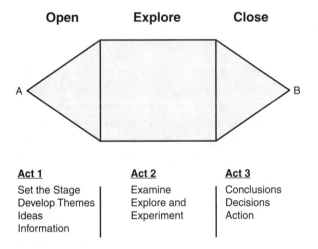

Figure 2-3 *Game Design*

In a game, a team wants to get from their known point A to fuzzy goal B, but they don't know how. So they apply this game framework to get there. We believe BDD includes this kind of game, with the same structure and accompanying mindsets. BDD is so much more than just this collaborative game, but this aspect of BDD is typically the hardest part for most teams to understand and master. Let's look at the three stages of the game structure.

Opening

The opening phase of the game is all about opening people's minds, opening up possibilities and ideas for later exploration. The opening is *divergent*, as illustrated in Figure 2-4. Generating new ideas is maximized and all critique is deliberately set aside. It's about getting as many ideas out in the open as possible and avoiding critical thinking and skepticism.

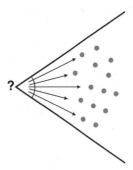

Figure 2-4 *Opening (Divergent)*

The opening stage in BDD involves brainstorming examples that help the team understand the business domain. These examples are focused on the customer experience and are as close as possible to the reality of the business domain. The goal is to generate a variety of examples that help the team understand the business domain and the customer need they are trying to address. Some teams split into pairs or triads to maximize the diversity of perspectives and ideas. This stage may take only a few minutes or much longer, depending on the complexity of the domain being considered.

Exploring

The keyword for the exploring stage is *emergent*. Exploration and experimentation are the focus. You want to create the conditions where "unexpected, surprising, and delightful things" emerge.[7] Figure 2-5 illustrates the nonlinear, emergent nature of the exploring stage.

In BDD, this stage builds on the energy and ideas that flowed into the room during the previous divergent stage, exploring the examples generated to see patterns and missing concepts and scenarios. If the team split into subgroups, this is when

---

7. *Gamestorming*, p. 11

the subgroups each take turns presenting their findings to the rest of the team, then the team looks for patterns, misunderstandings, missing concepts, and themes in the examples.

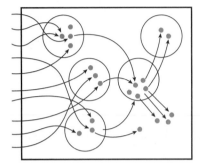

Figure 2-5 *Exploring (Emergent)*

The exploring stage can feel chaotic, directionless, and confusing to those not used to it. Thus, this stage can be very uncomfortable for teams that aren't used to exploring in this way. One facilitation book, the *Facilitator's Guide to Participatory Decision Making*, even refers to the exploring stage as "The Groan Zone," because the creative tension necessary for this stage takes effort to maintain and is discomforting for those not used to it.

Because of this tension, in the exploration stage of the game the temptation to critique options and converge on solutions as soon as possible can be very strong. If this happens, it can mean an early death to creativity, but this "groan zone" is a vital, normal, and necessary part of the creative process. Sam is used to formalizing proposed solutions early, which makes the exploration stage a big part of why he felt so uncomfortable playing the BDD game.

The right thing to do in exploration is to keep the creative tension and suspend judgment as long as necessary. This enables a team to pursue full participation, mutual understanding, inclusive solutions, and shared responsibility. We saw Jonah do this with the team, supporting and encouraging active dialogue about the various scenarios while not being afraid to dig a little deeper when necessary.

As we saw with the team, being very concrete is critical at this stage: who the user is in terms of background and experience, what they're trying to accomplish, what struggles they might have in getting their need met, where they are, and so on. All these kinds of details might seem quite incidental and unimportant, but they are vital in helping everyone visualize each scenario and identify what's missing, which then helps the team see other scenarios.

The focus in the exploration stage is on integrating the various ideas and perspectives rather than critiquing them. This is where the whole is greater than the sum of the parts. The team may analyze certain examples and discard them, or at least postpone further discussion on them. They may discover other examples that illuminate the domain more, and thus are pursued further. The team talks together about each example to make sure they understand it, filling in missing pieces and making note of things requiring further investigation.

Closing

The closing stage is where a game converges on conclusions, decisions, and action. It's finally the time to bring in critical thinking and rigor, evaluating which ideas are the most promising to pursue and worth an investment of time and energy. The keyword for this stage is *convergent*, as illustrated in Figure 2-6. It's about narrowing the field "in order to select the most promising things for whatever comes next."

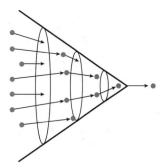

Figure 2-6 *Closing (Convergent)*

For the BDD "game," this means converging on a decision about which examples to carry through the rest of the BDD process. It involves starting to formalize the scenarios, looking for which details are significant and which are incidental. This leads us naturally to returning to our team in Chapter 3.

As we stated earlier, playing the BDD game is fundamentally about intentional discovery and growing a shared understanding. The overall BDD game structure looks like that shown in Figure 2-7, with divergent, emergent, and convergent stages.

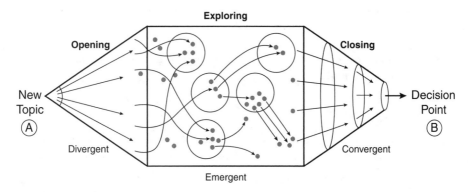

Figure 2-7 *BDD game structure*

Summary

- BDD is a collaborative game of exploring the desired behavior of a software system.

- People with different roles—usually product owner, developer, and tester—use examples to emerge this behavior rather than one individual trying to specify the behavior up front in isolation.

- Example mapping is a good technique for structuring a discussion around examples.

- Use real, concrete examples, not unrealistic dummy data.

- Use a common or happy path example to get to work on a real, concrete thing right away. Come back later to handle variations rather than trying to fully specify a story up front.

- Not everyone will be on board with trying a new way of working. Treat resistance as a resource, a source of information to engage rather than something to fight or avoid.

- Games like BDD have a natural structure—opening, exploring, and closing. Don't rush through the stages.

References

Cockburn, Alistair. *Agile Software Development: The Cooperative Game*. Boston: Pearson Education, Inc., 2007.

Emery, Dale H. "Resistance as a Resource." http://dhemery.com/articles/resistance _as_a_resource/

Gray, David, Sunni Brown, and James Macanufo. *Gamestorming: A Playbook for Innovators, Rulebreakers, and Changemakers*. Sebastopol, CA: O'Reilly, 2010.

Wynne, Matt. "Example Mapping": https://docs.cucumber.io/bdd/example-mapping/

Youngman, Dr. K. J. http://www.dbrmfg.co.nz/Bottom%20Line%20Agreement%20 to%20Change.htm

Chapter 3

Formalizing Examples into Scenarios

We prefer to separate the discovery step of BDD from the formalization and automation steps. Many teams get bogged down in trying to formalize examples too soon, rather than separating that out as a later task that can then be reviewed by the team.

Generating examples should be divergent and exploratory. As the team generates examples, the shape of the desired behavior emerges.

Formalizing examples is convergent. The team takes a single example and converges on a single precise set of words to describe it.

Rushing to formalization too quickly skips over important divergence and exploration.

In this chapter, we look at how to formalize examples into Cucumber scenarios using Cucumber's Gherkin language.

Moving from Examples to Scenarios

Second Whole Team Workshop, Later the Same Day

Setting: The team conference room in the library's downtown office. (MARK, ROBIN, RAJ, SAM, JESSIE, JANE, and JONAH are sitting around the conference table, chatting as RAJ finishes firing up the projector.)

RAJ: OK, here we are, Robin and I took a little time after lunch with Jonah to create an initial draft of the Cucumber feature file to discuss now.

So, I've got the ebook search feature file up on the screen for us, can everyone see that clearly?

ALL: Yes.

```
Feature: Search for an ebook by title
  Library patron searches library catalog for a specific ebook
  so she can read it on her Kindle

  * Assume the library has the book in our catalog

  Scenario: Find an ebook for my Kindle by the exact title
    Given I am on the library catalog search page
    When I search for "Words of Radiance"
    Then I should see the following book at the top of my search results:
      | Name        | Words of Radiance |
      | Author      | Brandon Sanderson |
      | Call Number | FIC SANDERSO B    |
      | Format      | Mobi              |

  Scenario: Search for an ebook for my Kindle where the title doesn't
  ➥ exactly match
    Given I am on the library catalog search page
    When I search for "Word of Radiance"
    Then I should see the following book somewhere in my search results:

  Scenario: Search for an ebook for my Kindle but don't have it in that
  ➥ format

  # Placeholder - need to discuss
  Scenario: Search for an ebook for my Kindle but don't have it at all in
  ➥ the catalog
```

JONAH: Thanks, Raj. As Raj mentioned, we took the notes from this morning's meeting and wrote them up in this feature file. This is just a first draft, but there's enough there now that it was worth sharing and refining together.

JANE: It looks a lot like a test plan to me. The kind of thing I would typically write after Raj and Robin have handed the feature over to me to test.

JONAH: You're right, it does function somewhat as a test plan. What similarities do you see?

JANE: Well, I see several scenarios that describe the feature we're discussing, the way we want the feature to behave, and each line in the scenario is a step in verifying the behavior for that scenario. That's just like my test plans, which I usually write in Word documents.

I also tend to put in placeholders for tests until I can figure out exactly what the right steps for verifying the correct behavior should be, just like we've done here.

I usually put in specific examples in my test plans too, though I wouldn't normally talk about that with anyone else like we have for this file. I also put in a lot of details about what needs to be clicked in the UI so I remember what I need to do each time I manually step through it.

This is just a plain text file, right?

JONAH: Yes, correct.

The big difference with this, as you said, is that we're doing it now, prior to starting coding. We collaborate together on the examples to use for the feature file, and then we create it *before* Raj and Robin start coding up the feature.

I tend to think of a feature file more as a *collaboration point*, as a springboard for conversation and discovery. The test automation that comes later is a nice side effect of growing these feature files as a kind of "living documentation."

JANE: Does this mean that my test plans go away completely? I'll still do some manual testing, right?

JONAH: Teams doing BDD typically focus the manual testing they do on exploratory testing, on testing the things that fall outside of what the feature file covers.

Since you do test plans now, I suggest you continue following your current practice if it's working for you. Once you get used to using feature files more, I suspect you'll see areas in which you can make improvements to how you approach your testing. That's something to reflect on in future retros.

JANE: Makes sense. It will be great to have more time for exploratory testing.

MARK: Seems straightforward enough to me, too.

JANE: Yes, I'll be interested in seeing where it goes from here. Seems like this approach should reduce a lot of the monkey work I have to do and push the testing much earlier into each sprint, since we'll be doing a lot of it as we go.

ROBIN: I'm confused, so you're saying a feature file is a *test plan*? I thought the feature file was the way we specify how a feature should work. Or am I missing something here?

JONAH: A feature file is not a test plan. What I meant was that some of the things Jane's current test plans accomplish will now happen via running the feature files in Cucumber.

You are right: A feature file specifies how a feature should work, so it functions as an executable specification for the feature so you know what to code. It's more than that, though. It also assumes some responsibility for checking that, after you implement the production code, the feature does actually work the way it should. This is the test automation piece, which we'll be getting to later, once we have a feature file we can automate.

SAM: I get it, you're saying we should get all our feature files formalized in the first step, then do the test automation as a later step. Makes sense to me.

JONAH: I can see how you might get that from what I'm saying, but I'm not talking about treating exploration, formalization, and automation in BDD as separate phases. They are just steps each feature goes through. Sam, it seems to me you're thinking of it as a linear approach, but it's not.

What I am saying is that it's helpful to have a different *mindset* and approach for each step when doing BDD. When exploring examples, you're in a discovery mindset, trying to understand the domain and uncover what assumptions you might have that are incorrect. When formalizing examples, you need to start introducing some rigor around terminology, around the business language you use. When writing feature files, you're trying to drive out ambiguity and incidental details and make sure you're all on the same page with how each feature should work. This will become clearer as we dig into it more.

SAM: I'm not sure I get it but, as you said, let's keep going and hopefully it will be a bit clearer to me.

ROBIN: Jonah, I think I get it. One other question: Should we start using Cucumber for all our automated testing? I've talked to a lot of developers who tried Cucumber and gave up on it. They said the specs were too brittle and slow, and there was just too much overhead. I'm not wanting to be overly negative here, but these are smart people who seemed to know what they were talking about.

JONAH: It's true, a lot of teams try Cucumber and give up on it for the exact reasons you describe. There's a lot I could say about that, but maybe it's sufficient for now to say I'm pretty sure they were trying to use Cucumber just as an automated test runner rather than as a collaboration tool. They were probably writing scenarios for things that would be better handled with their regular unit testing framework, like RSpec or JUnit. Cucumber does introduce overhead with the feature files, but that overhead is worth it when you use the tool for the purposes for which it was intended. It's first and foremost a collaboration tool.

It's hard to explain these things until we actually get into them. These are common points of confusion, so don't lose heart.

There's a model I like for thinking about the different types of testing activities Agile teams do. I've found it can be helpful to see where BDD fits in to the rest of what you do.

Feature Files as Collaboration Points

As we begin formalizing examples, BDD begins to look more like testing. Let's see how it relates to other testing activities. In *Agile Testing*, Lisa Crispin and Janet Gregory described a model for thinking about the various kinds of testing in Agile software development, which they called the "Agile Testing Quadrants," shown in Figure 3-1.

The vertical axis in this model describes whose perspective is taken in the tests. Business-facing tests are tests from the business or customer perspective. They ask questions about whether the system does the functions it ought to do. Technology-facing tests are tests from the developer or team perspective. They ask questions about the implementation: Does the code do what developers intend? Does the system perform well? Is it secure? Of course, customers care about things like performance, but they rarely understand performance tests, and the tests often depend on knowledge of implementation details.

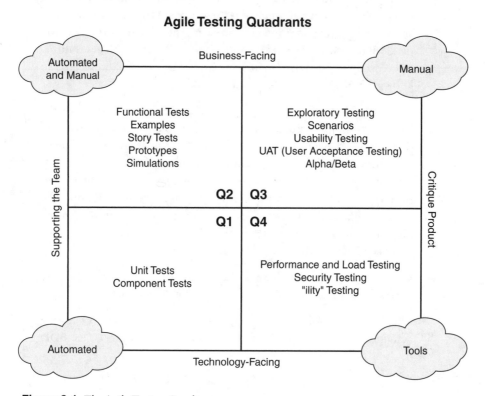

Figure 3-1 *The Agile Testing Quadrants*

The horizontal axis in the model describes when tests are executed relative to development and what function they serve. Tests that critique the product look at something that already exists in order to ask questions about what it does or how it does it. This is what we traditionally think of as testing. On the other side, tests that support the team are tests used to drive development. These tests are written before the software that will make them pass. They act as specifications for features and code.

As we saw in the dialogue, creating an initial draft of a feature file is the first step toward formalizing the examples harvested from the team conversations. As the team talks about the business domain, they seek to understand what the behavior of the system should be in response to the customer's needs. They distill these examples into scenarios in the feature file.

Such examples provide structure and focus to specification, but that's only half the story: Those examples become test scenarios so the team can get automated feedback about the state of the system.

Let's look at how BDD with Cucumber relates to other kinds of testing an Agile team might do based on the Agile Testing Quadrants model.

- **Quadrant 1: Technology-facing tests that support the team:** Quadrant 1 contains technology-facing tests that support the team as it develops the software. This is what we typically think of as test-driven development, or TDD. In TDD, a developer writes a small unit test describing the next bit of code she'd like to create. She runs the test and confirms that it fails, that it describes something not true of the code right now. Then, she writes just enough code to make the test pass. Assuming all previous tests continue to pass, she either refactors the code to improve its design without changing its behavior or writes the next failing unit test. Quadrant 1 tests are automated; they're run many, many times in the course of development and must be fast and easy to use.

  In the course of making a single Cucumber scenario pass, a developer using TDD will typically write many unit tests. TDD is a small loop inside the bigger BDD loop.

- **Quadrant 4: Technology-facing tests that critique the product:** Quadrant 4 tests cover what are typically referred to as "nonfunctional requirements," such as performance, security, scalability, and so on. These tests ask questions about a product or increment of product that already has been developed. Often, such tests require a dedicated, production-like test environment, making them difficult to execute during development. Nonetheless, teams should find ways to get this feedback early and often lest they discover a problem too late to do anything about it. Quadrant 4 tests may be automated. Even when they're not automated, they're typically tool-assisted.

  Quadrant 4 tests usually address different concerns from Cucumber scenarios. Together, they describe the system more fully.

- **Quadrant 3: Business-facing tests that critique the product:** This is the work typically done by people with "tester" or "QA" in their job title. They look at a product or product increment that already exists and ask questions about whether it does what it ought to do. They look for edge cases, boundary conditions, and defects. Quadrant 3 tests tend to be manual. They ask questions that were not anticipated by automated tests.

  Failing Quadrant 3 tests often become new Cucumber scenarios to drive the necessary development to make those tests pass.

- **Quadrant 2: Business-facing tests that support the team:** BDD fits in Quadrant 2. In Quadrant 2, tests address the behavior of the system from the business perspective. Unlike Quadrant 3 tests, however, Quadrant 2 tests are written *before* the code that makes them pass, and thus are used as a tool to write that code correctly. Quadrant 2 tests are executable examples acting as functional specifications.

Mapping Your Current Testing Activities

Consider the testing activities your team currently does. How do they map to the quadrants? Do you do any testing to support the team, or do all your tests critique the product? If your developers write unit tests but not until after the code exists, you don't do Quadrant 1 tests—those unit tests aren't supporting the team during development. If you're like many Agile teams, you have decent coverage of Quadrant 3, some activity in Quadrant 4, occasional Quadrant 1, and nothing in Quadrant 2.

How Will Adopting BDD Affect Your Testing?

By adopting BDD, you will fill in more of Quadrant 2, allowing testers to do more interesting tests in Quadrant 3 and perhaps dedicate more time to Quadrant 4. In the process, you'll be investing in creating a foundation and motivation for the adoption of developer-facing TDD to fill in Quadrant 1.

Quadrant 2 tests can create a foundation for moving into Quadrant 1. They build a safety net for the refactoring most teams need to do to make their code more testable in small units. They teach the test-first approach in a way that's easy to understand, and they create motivation for more attention to be paid to Quadrant 1 because Quadrant 2 tests are inevitably larger and slower. Once teams become accustomed to automated tests supporting their development, they want faster, more granular tests. Eventually, each Quadrant 2 test will drive the development of multiple Quadrant 1 tests as part of developing the code.

In the dialogues, our library team is currently working on Quadrant 2 tests with Cucumber. The scenarios so far test the new ebook search behavior from the user's perspective. In the next chapter, they'll begin automating these scenarios. The automation will drive the library website, which is realistic but relatively slow. Raj and Robin might decide they want faster feedback on a part of the ebook search engine as they develop it. This will motivate them to create smaller, faster unit tests for themselves (Quadrant 1).

Growing Quadrant 2 Collaboration Capabilities

A feature file is a Quadrant 2 collaboration point; a springboard for conversation and discovery. The Quadrant 2 test automation that comes later is a nice side effect of growing these feature files as a species of "living documentation." This is in contrast to a test plan, which is typically a step-by-step description of how a particular feature is going to be verified as having the correct behavior.

The Perils of Misusing Cucumber

Cucumber is a Quadrant 2 collaboration tool. This means that scenarios ought to take the user's perspective and developers ought to involve product people—business stakeholders, product owners, business analysts—in creating and reviewing scenarios.

Some teams make the mistake of using Cucumber exclusively as a Quadrant 1 developer-facing tool. This leads to unnecessary technical overhead, brittle and slow test scenarios, and eventually unmaintainable feature files. The value is simply not there when treating Cucumber as a developer-facing tool.

In "The World's Most Misunderstood Collaboration Tool," Cucumber creator Aslak Hellesoy acknowledges that Cucumber's unique value is as a collaboration tool, not as a pure test automation tool:

> There is a certain amount of ceremony involved with Cucumber. There is both Gherkin and Step Definitions to maintain. This can be justified if it improves collaboration and reduces misunderstandings, but if the tool is used in a vacuum those benefits will obviously never happen.[1]

The same is true when using Cucumber predominantly as a Quadrant 3 tool by employing the same test-after approach used in many enterprise test tools or other open-source automation tools like Selenium. In this case, scenarios tend to look like manual test plans. They describe how a tester would test a behavior rather than specifying what a user wants the behavior to be.

Teams Already Doing Lots of Quadrant 3 Testing

If your team does mostly Quadrant 3 testing, where the bulk of your testing is done (manual or automated) *after* the software has been written, what are your options? Some teams write detailed test plan documents for activities in this quadrant, whereas many teams take a more ad hoc approach. Some teams create many automated tests to verify the software after it has been written, while the vast majority of teams focus on manual testing. BDD with Cucumber has a place for each of these situations.

---

1. https://cucumber.io/blog/2014/03/03/the-worlds-most-misunderstood-collaboration-tool

Jane writes test plans, which is unusual for most Agile teams. However, development teams working in heavily regulated industries, such as in medical device software development, are typically required by regulations to produce detailed documentation and to work within a higher-ceremony process. We find that, even in regulated environments, Cucumber features can frequently replace formal test plans and other artifacts like traceability matrices. (Development teams will often have to negotiate this change with their compliance people. A period of producing both test plans and Cucumber features for the same behavior might be necessary to prove that both artifacts do the same job for regulatory compliance.)

Rather than waiting to hand-write test plan documents after each new piece of functionality is ready to test and then manually testing the functionality, teams using Cucumber can collaboratively define the expected behavior using concrete examples in feature files, and the programmers can implement the functionality to make the scenarios pass. Rather than using a serial, manual, "throw functionality over the wall" process, coders and testers can work together to understand, implement, and verify the requirements.

Teams writing test plans after the fact typically benefit as testers begin to collaborate in all aspects of the development process, including specifying the product behavior, development, testing, and deployment. Testers bring a unique perspective and expertise that's useful throughout development.

Teams taking a less formal approach by doing all their testing manually with no documentation at all may expect Cucumber to introduce more overhead. As we've mentioned, if they don't also start doing BDD and using Cucumber as a collaboration tool, this is exactly what will happen. Feature files don't replace manual testing; they supplement it. The subsequent test automation takes away much of the repetitive, manual work from testing, enabling testers to focus more attention on ensuring the whole team is "getting the software right."

Feature files don't replace manual testing, and teams may still get value from writing some test plans to augment the feature files by describing things that must be tested manually due to high overhead or complexity in test automation. We're not saying teams with a more ad hoc specification and testing approach should be writing test plan documents but rather that feature files serve double duty as executable specifications, providing a greater level of rigor for teams currently lacking more rigorous testing efforts.

Another thing to keep in mind is that because feature files are plain text, it is common for teams to store them in their version control system (that is, Subversion, Mercurial, or Git) as part of their source code, giving the team a full version history. This enables teams to document and track changes to their executable documentation and collaborate on changes should there ever be merge conflicts.

The Whole Team Workshop Continues to Refine the Scenario

JONAH: Since you're all learning together, I suggest we walk through the happy path example here and focus our time now on getting that one as right as we can make it, based on what we know now. That's why we mostly left placeholders for the rest of the scenarios.

Once we get this happy path scenario where we want it, which shouldn't take too long, Raj and Robin can then go away and write the automation piece for it. They'll write some automation code for each step, what we call the "step definitions," so we can actually use this scenario to drive the web browser as tests for the ebook scenario.

JANE: Glad to hear that. Almost all the testing I do now is completely manual, based on the test plans I mentioned. We've got some browser automation in place; there are Selenium tests that Raj helped me write last year in one area, but it's very limited. It will be nice to have Raj and Robin take point on the automation piece and drive features going forward.

JONAH: Definitely. Test automation is real software development, so it makes sense for developers to be involved in it.

SAM: I'm looking at that scenario…

```
Feature: Search for an ebook by title
  Library patron searches library catalog for a specific ebook
  so she can read it on her Kindle

  * Assume the library has the book in our catalog

  Scenario: Find an ebook for my Kindle by the exact title
    Given I am on the library catalog search page
    When I search for "Words of Radiance"
    Then I should see the following book at the top of my search results:
      | Name        | Words of Radiance |
      | Author      | Brandon Sanderson |
      | Call Number | FIC SANDERSO B    |
      | Format      | Mobi              |
```

What's the syntax mean, then? Why does each step start with "Given," "When," or "Then?" Are those special words?

JONAH: Yes, they are part of the syntax of the Cucumber language, called *Gherkin*, for feature files. I recommend you don't worry too much about the syntax at this point. We'll dig into that more at a later time, and there are some great reference guides I can point you to on how to write good feature files.

Let's focus on the content for now rather than on the syntax, format, or layout. You can see we put a description of the feature at the top of the file, under the feature name: *(Reads)*

```
Library patron searches library catalog for a specific ebook
so she can read it on her Kindle
```

This description is optional in the feature file, but I find it helpful for getting the bigger picture. It makes the feature file function more like a living specification: Now anyone reading this in the future will know why this feature is important and what it does. Mark, did we capture it adequately?

MARK: Looks good to me.

JONAH: Great. You'll also all see we put a note in there for the first scenario saying we are assuming the book is in the catalog, as we discussed earlier. We could have made that a comment with a hash character instead of the asterisk, but comments don't show up in the output from running the scenarios, and I think it's important to make that assumption transparent.

ROBIN: Mark, as Raj and I were putting this together with Jonah, I wanted to see how the current catalog works now, so I went to our main public search page and searched for "Words of Radiance" just like we had discussed this morning. Incidentally, I see what you meant about the problems with the current search; there were all kinds of things in the results.

Anyway, obviously we don't have the Kindle edition in our catalog yet, but we were able to see the kind of book information we listed in the scenario: Name, Author, Call Number, and Format. Jonah explained that Cucumber feature files can have nice tables in them like this one, so doing that helped us clean up the layout from what we had initially.

JESSIE: What's "Mobi" again?

MARK: Mobi is the Kindle format. Technically, it is Mobi, but that's not how patrons are going to talk about that. Most Kindle owners don't know that the format is Mobi.

JESSIE: OK, so in terms of user experience, it's not Mobi, it's Kindle. I'll make sure our mockup has that correct.

JANE: What do you think we will do for the HTML markup, which one will it be?

RAJ: *(Updating the feature file on the screen)* We'll display "Kindle" on the page.

JESSIE: Right.

JANE: Hmm...I'm thinking I'll need to do some extra testing around the actual format to make sure it's Mobi for the download.

JONAH: Good catch, Jessie and Mark. I think we're pretty much there with this first one. Jane, that sounds like a great idea, how about you and Raj discuss that later?

JANE: No problem.

JONAH: Anyone else spot anything we missed or need to tweak?

SAM: Well, if I understand this story correctly, we're not actually going from the library catalog search page; the starting point is actually the ebook search page. You know, the ebook menu option at the top of the page. So, shouldn't it say something like, "Given I am on the ebook search page"?

MARK: Right.

JONAH: Actually, the scenario really doesn't need to talk about pages at all. As far as the user is concerned, they're just searching for an ebook. So, we can drop the Given step and just say something like "When I search ebooks for..."

RAJ: *(Makes the changes)* OK, got it.

JONAH: Raj, before we forget, how about you put another note in the feature description about the Mobi format thing, so we capture that for later?

RAJ: How's this?

```
* Assume the library has the book in our catalog
* Kindle books are Mobi format

Scenario: Find an ebook for my Kindle by the exact title
  When I search ebooks for "Words of Radiance"
  Then I should see the following book at the top of my search results:
    | Name        | Words of Radiance |
    | Author      | Brandon Sanderson |
    | Call Number | FIC SANDERSO B    |
    | Format      | Mobi              |
```

MARK: Looks fine to me.

SAM: Wait, we don't need a `Given` step?

JONAH: No, we can go straight to the When step if there's nothing to say about the context before the user takes an action.

Looks like the first scenario is good enough to automate. Raj, how about you and I pair up after this and work through that?

RAJ: OK. We can head back to my desk afterward.

JONAH: Great. OK, let's walk through the rest, not to get them to the same level of detail at this point but to make sure we capture the main details.

SAM: What's this next one: "Search for an ebook for my Kindle where the title doesn't exactly match"? I don't remember talking about it this morning.

ROBIN: As Raj and I ran through the first scenario using the current catalog search, I forgot the "s" in "Words" and we discovered that our book *Words of Radiance* didn't even show up in the current search results at all. It should show up, though, right?

MARK: Absolutely.

ROBIN: So we realized that was the kind of thing that would be happening for our library patrons, too. We added a scenario about partial matches that we hadn't previously talked about so we could discuss it with you all.

MARK: Sounds good to me. This should be the way our new feature works.

ROBIN: Great. We also weren't sure about "Search for an ebook for my Kindle but don't have it in that format." We just put a placeholder there so we could see what you all think. Do we need to handle this scenario?

JESSIE: I don't understand what you mean. Are you saying the library patron searches for *Words of Radiance* but we only have hard copies in our catalog?

ROBIN: It could be, but we were thinking more about having it as an epub. It's when you search for *Words of Radiance* and we have it in epub but not in Kindle, so it's a different digital format. Maybe the scenario should have been: "Search for an ebook for my Kindle but only have it in non-Kindle format," or "...only have it in epub format." Or something like that.

MARK: I see. I'm not sure about this one, we'll likely need to handle it at a later date, so maybe we should include it now.

JONAH: Mark, how well does this non-Kindle format scenario fit into our MMF?

MARK: Hmm...it doesn't really. We did agree to focus only on Kindles at this time. At least for this first MMF.

JONAH: Right. I suggest we try to narrow our focus at this point if we can, rather than take on additional scenarios. And if this one doesn't fit into the MMF as Mark said, I suggest we split it out into a different story so we can really only focus on Kindle for this first MMF. After all, it is meant to be a "minimal" marketable feature. Better to get this first Kindle MMF done sooner so we can get user feedback on the feature before moving on to other formats.

MARK: You're right, Jonah. It's tempting to put this in as well, but I'll add something to the backlog for later.

Describing Features

Some teams prefer to have the feature description be in the common user story format, "As a [role], I want to ... etc.," rather than a free-form description of the feature. Capturing who, what, and why for a feature is a good idea. However, Cucumber features aren't user stories; Cucumber features are living documentation of a set of behaviors in the system. A single feature may grow and change over the course of many user stories.

To avoid confusion between Cucumber features and user stories, simply describe the feature. Treat the feature file as living documentation and incorporate the documentation of the feature into the actual feature file. If you can, include information on the user's role and the benefit or driver for the feature. Also provide any background information on the feature that might be helpful, such as details about the business domain and definitions of any important domain terms.

Using MMFs *with BDD Can Keep You from Generating an* Excess *of Examples*

Notice that the team decided to throw away an example instead of adding it to the feature file as a new scenario. That example was not part of the MMF they were working on, so the team was able to postpone covering that example and refocus on the work at hand. Remember, MMFs are a tool to get earlier value and feedback. To achieve this benefit, MMFs need to stay minimal.

Some teams find it difficult to restrict their conversations to appropriate examples, not having a sound understanding of whether they should be digging in to it. Someone proposes an example, with perhaps "what if...happens?" and the team spends an inordinate amount of time digging into a case that ultimately could be deferred until later. MMFs provide a way to avoid that situation. The person facilitating the conversation can say something like, "That sounds like a case we'll definitely need to cover, but it's not part of this MMF. Let's put it on our parking lot or backlog and cover it later."

Collaborating for Understanding

Someone might say, "This team seems to spend a lot of time in meetings. When do they get the actual work done?" It's easy to think that typing code into an editor is the actual work of software development and that everything else around it is a distraction from the work. Compounding that perception is the fact that many software developers are much more comfortable spending time with their computers than with other humans, so the coding part of the work also feels more pleasant.

The work of a software development team isn't creating software, it's solving people's problems with software. Thus, understanding the problem and how to best solve it is a critical part of the work. The meetings you're seeing from the library team in this book are cross-functional collaboration, at the center of what the team's trying to accomplish.

This is not to say that all meetings are valuable. Meetings have gotten a bad rap for good reason: There are lots of wasteful, ineffective meetings.

In some organizations, we noticed that the word *meeting* specifically refers to the bad kind of meeting. You might see this in a Daily Scrum. If someone says, "Yesterday, I went to the meeting," they probably consider that wasted time. If it was valuable, they'll say something like, "Yesterday, I worked with Ann and Ramu to flesh out the user experience." Objectively, that collaboration happened in a meeting, but because *meeting* has come to mean wasting time with other people in a conference room, good meetings are remembered as just getting stuff done.

That's fine, we have no attachment to the word *meeting*, but we sure see a lot of value in people collaborating to build the right software. In this book, we've tried to illustrate what that collaboration might look like.

In particular, take note of how each meeting has a clear purpose, how it stays focused on that purpose, and how the team transitions between larger and smaller conversations depending on what they're doing.

Wrapping Up the Whole Team Workshop

MARK: I like that we have this last one: "Search for an ebook for my Kindle but don't have it at all in the catalog" is important.

ROBIN: Thanks. Raj pointed that one out. What should happen? We figured there needed to be some kind of message, like "Item not found in catalog," but we weren't sure if that's right.

JESSIE: Our current catalog says: "Zero items found." That's been a pet peeve of mine for a long time. I've wanted us to have something a little more informative, like what Robin just suggested.

MARK: Agreed. Robin, let's go with your suggestion for now.

RAJ: *(Typing)* OK, we've got a comment in there about this.

JONAH: Good enough for now, I think. Though, Mark, what would be a good example of an ebook that would not be in the catalog?

MARK: Hmmm. Let's use *The Whole Library Handbook*, since I know it's only available in paperback.

JONAH: Great, thanks.

SAM: Aren't we going to finish these other scenarios right now? I'd rather capture all the details in this meeting in this feature file and make sure it's clean. You know, treat it like a real spec.

JONAH: Yes, we want to get it clean. And we'll definitely get it to the level you're expecting. For now, let's hold off on getting the feature file finished until we've got some experience with taking a scenario through the whole loop of exploration, formalization, and automation. The first scenario is ready to automate, and we've got the main ideas there for the rest. Raj has been taking notes in the comments around the scenarios.

So, how about two or three of us go off and formalize it and clean it up as an offline activity rather than tie up this meeting dictating to the person at the keyboard? Then we can regroup later to review the automation of the first scenario and the formalization of the rest.

SAM: OK.

JANE: Sam and Robin, how about we get some practice cleaning up this file? Since we finished this meeting a little early, I have some time before our next one.

SAM: Sure. We can use my office if Robin brings her laptop.

ROBIN: Works for me.

RAJ: Robin, I've just checked in our changes so far so you can pull them down onto your laptop.

MARK: Sounds good to me, too. I've got my next meeting to get ready for anyway. Let's get together here tomorrow morning at 9 a.m. to review our progress here in this same room.

JONAH: What do you think, Raj? You up for writing some step definitions?

RAJ: Yes. I need to reply to a couple of pressing emails at my desk, then I'll have the rest of the afternoon to pair with you.

JONAH: Excellent. Well, thanks everyone. Raj, I'll swing by in about 15 minutes. Sam, Jessie, and Robin, I expect it won't take you long to formalize those other scenarios, but let me know if you get stuck or would like any feedback.

RAJ: OK. See you then.

ROBIN: Will do!

BDD Is Iterative, Not Linear

In the previous dialogue Sam confused different mindsets and steps of BDD with phases. He wanted to work on the feature file once, polish it, and move on. There's a temptation, particularly for development teams used to a waterfall software lifecycle, to mistake BDD for a linear process. They see that BDD involves exploration, formalization, and automation steps and mistake this for a serial process. However, this could not be further from the truth. The reality is that teams using BDD refine and improve their feature files over time as they explore and learn.

At any point, a team may switch from one step to another. They might be formalizing a scenario in their feature file and realize they need to jump back into exploration because they've uncovered a case they hadn't thought about, and need to talk about examples to drive better understanding. The same thing can happen when automating scenarios. While automating one scenario, new scenarios might present themselves or further exploration of examples might need to happen.

It might be confusing in the dialogue where we had the team leave placeholders for the rest of the scenarios. Perhaps you're wondering, "Shouldn't we be trying to get the feature file correct and complete as soon as possible?" Most teams tend to create an initial cut of a feature file to use as a conversation starter, then iterate and refine it over time as they learn new things. For a well-understood domain, the first cut of the feature file might be sufficient. Some teams start with the first example and take it through the entire flow of formalizing it as a scenario, then automating the tests as they proceed to implement the actual production code.

Jonah says to "focus on the content for now rather than the syntax, format, or layout." Does this mean Gherkin isn't important? No, we're not saying that at all. Gherkin is important, but there is a time and a place for formalization. Jonah dissuaded the team from formalizing the scenarios in this meeting because formalizing feature files as a group is a brain-numbing activity. It can feel like a group of people all writing an essay together. Better to take that offline, have one or two people work on it, and then return to present the results to the other participants to get their feedback on errors and omissions.

Robin and Raj tried the current catalog search and found a new scenario around "partial matches." This is typical of the iterative rather than linear nature of BDD. As Robin and Raj were exploring the domain by investigating the current system functionality, they learned something new and incorporated it into their draft of the feature file as a reminder to review it with other team members to get clarity on it.

Finding the Meaningful Variations

Once you have the happy path scenario, how do you come up with the meaningful variations that will make your scenarios expressive and your user story complete without getting buried in noise?

There are some heuristics, a bit of art, and a lot of collaboration in making this work. We tend to go through a series of questions to ourselves like these:

- Where are all the places where things could be different in the happy path? In other words, what are the *variables/variations*?

- Which variable is most likely to change?

- What's an example of a change that causes a different outcome? What's another change that causes a different outcome?

- Where are the boundaries of that change? Explore both sides.

- What could go wrong? Is there value for one of the variables that breaks something? What should happen?

Repeat for other variables.

Testers are particularly good at identifying possible variations, but you need the product owner perspective to evaluate whether a particular example is relevant and valuable. In exploratory testing, it's great when testers consider variations no one else has thought of. However, because feature files function as living documentation of the behavior of the system, we don't want to clutter that documentation with unlikely edge cases.

Occasionally, a variation is worth covering with an automated test but isn't one the product owner cares about. Cover these variations with developer-facing unit tests.

Gherkin: A Language for Expressive Scenarios

Jonah advised the team early on not to worry too much about the syntax of the Cucumber language, called *Gherkin*, for feature files. We're going to provide a guide to the Gherkin keywords and syntax, but first we'll talk a little about what kind of language Cucumber speaks.

A *pidgin language* is a simplified language used for communication between two or more groups that do not have a common language. A key element of a pidgin language is that it develops for a particular shared goal across those language groups, usually trade. It's not just a new language; it's a new language optimized for a purpose. Cucumber's language for describing features is called Gherkin, and Gherkin is a pidgin language for describing the behavior of a software system in a way both humans and their computers can understand.

Gherkin is a simplified language for programmers, testers, and product people to collaboratively describe examples of business scenarios and thus define the expected system behavior. Gherkin provides a small set of terms and sufficient structure to enable your team to write scenarios rich with business domain language with minimal effort. It's neither a full-fledged programming language like Java nor a complete human language like English, and that's intentional.

Feature Title and Description

Cucumber features always begin with the `Feature` keyword (or the equivalent in another human language) and a feature title. This can be followed by text describing the feature. This text can be whatever you like; for example:

```
Feature: Library patron account reinstatement following full fee payment
  When a library patron's card is blocked she cannot check out or renew materials.
  Payment of all fees reinstates her account.
```

or as we saw in the dialogue above,

```
Feature: Search for an ebook by title
  Library patron searches library catalog for a specific ebook
  so she can read it on her Kindle
```

Cucumber treats any text between the feature title and the first `Scenario` or `Background` keyword as the description.

Scenarios and `Given-When-Then`

The core of the Gherkin language is the *scenario*, a concrete example of a feature in action. Scenarios begin with the `Scenario` keyword followed by a title and are specified as a sequence of steps that each start with the keyword `Given`, `When`, `Then`, `And`, or `But`.

```
Scenario: Reinstate deactivated account
  Given a library patron owes $13.05 in unpaid fees and fines
  When she pays the full amount
  Then she should have no fines and fees
  And her library card should be unblocked
```

A `When` step describes the main action being taken in the scenario. There should be only one `When` step per scenario. A `Then` step asserts something about the state of the system after the `When` step changes the system state in some way. A `Given` step sets up the context required to execute the `When` step.

It's common to see the same `When` step used for multiple scenarios in a feature alongside different `Given` and `Then` steps—taking the same action in a different context often yields different results. For example:

```
Scenario: Admins can edit catalog items
  Given I'm logged in as an administrator
  When I go to the catalog page
  Then I should see an edit link by each catalog item

Scenario: Non-admins can't edit catalog items
  Given I'm logged in as a regular user
  When I go to the catalog page
  Then I should not see an edit link by any catalog item
```

The scenario title should be short, usually no more than five or six words, and it should express what makes this scenario different from the others in the feature. Test results will render the scenario titles under the feature title like an outline, so scenario titles need not repeat information already covered by the feature title.

Multiline String Step Arguments

Sometimes a step needs more data than can be provided on a single line. For example:

```
When I create a catalog item with the description:
  """
  Lorem ipsum dolor sit amet, consectetur adipiscing elit.
  Ut et ipsum turpis, sodales convallis nulla. Vestibulum
  iaculis sodales felis in ultrices. Vestibulum dapibus
  lobortis facilisis. Nulla vel orci vel nulla mattis viverra.
  Nam vitae mauris mattis lectus pellentesque semper non eu
  diam. Aenean elementum nisi at dui iaculis semper.
  """
```

The three double quotes before and after the block of dummy Latin text indicate a multiline string step argument. This value will be passed as a last argument to the matching step definition. (Remember from the earlier dialogue, step definitions are the bits of code that run for each Gherkin step when you run the scenario.)

The colon at the end of the step isn't required by Cucumber. It's just a convention we like to use to tell human readers to keep reading for the rest of the step.

Table Step Arguments

Sometimes a step needs more data than can be provided on a single line, and that data can be structured into a table. For example:

```
Given the following library patrons:
  | Name         | Email                     |
  | Chandra Khan | chandra@somedomain.com    |
  | Denise Jones | denise@anotherdomain.com  |
```

Tables are indicated by pipe characters around the table cells. As with multiline string arguments, the table will be passed as the last argument to the matching step definition, but it will be a Cucumber table object rather than a string.

Sometimes it can be convenient to create a table representing key-value pairs, especially when you need to perform an operation that requires too much data to easily be represented in a sentence-like step. For example:

```
When I search for a catalog item with advanced search criteria:
  | Item Type     | Book               |
  | Subject       | endangered species |
  | General Notes | history            |
  | Author        | McClung            |
  | Publisher     | Hamden             |
```

Notice that this table has no header row; each row contains data. Or, more precisely, the table is rotated with headers in the left column and data in the right column.

Tables aren't just useful for setting up data or performing complex operations. They are also good for Then steps where you want to assert about a set of data. The preceding book search step might be followed by a step like this:

```
Then the results should contain the following catalog item:
  | Title            | Call Number         |
  | LOST WILD AMERICA | Y591.529097 McClung |
```

Or it could use the key-value table format, depending on what is most expressive in the context of a particular set of scenarios:

```
Then the results should contain the following catalog item:
  | Title       | LOST WILD AMERICA   |
  | Call Number | Y591.529097 McClung |
```

Fortunately, we don't need to compare the actual and expected values ourselves. Cucumber's table object has a diff method, which will do the comparison and tell us about nonmatching, missing, and surplus values. Cucumber's online documentation covers tables in detail.[2]

---

2. https://docs.cucumber.io/

Gherkin provides a lot of flexibility when specifying data in your steps. For example, you could phrase the same step several different ways:

```
When I search for call numbers starting with Y591, Y592, Y593, Y594
```

or

```
When I search for call numbers starting with:
  | Y591 |
  | Y592 |
  | Y593 |
  | Y594 |
```

The first example works nicely if you have only a few values to pass through, while the second makes it easier to pass more values.

Background

When you find yourself reusing the same `Given` steps in every scenario, you can use a `Background` section to remove that duplication. Steps in the `Background` section run before each scenario, just as if they were part of every scenario in the feature. So, for example, the following:

```
Feature: Administrative functions

  Scenario: Admins can edit catalog items
    Given I'm logged in as an administrator
    When I go to the catalog page
    Then I should see an edit link by each catalog item

  Scenario: Only certain catalog item fields are editable
    Given I'm logged in as an administrator
    When I edit a catalog item
    Then I should see the following fields:
      | Item Type     |
      | Subject       |
      | General notes |
      | Author        |
      | Publisher     |
```

becomes

```
Feature: Administrative functions

  Background:
    Given I'm logged in as an administrator
```

```
Scenario: Admins can edit catalog items
  When I go to the catalog page
  Then I should see an edit link by each catalog item

Scenario: Only certain catalog item fields are editable
  When I edit a catalog item
  Then I should see the following fields:
    | Item Type     |
    | Subject       |
    | General notes |
    | Author        |
    | Publisher     |
```

and runs exactly the same.

Scenario Outlines

When you find yourself reusing the same steps with different data in multiple scenarios, a Scenario Outline block is a great way to remove the duplicated steps and put the focus on the variations in data.

The following scenarios differ only in their data:

```
Scenario: Search for "BDD with Cucumber"
  Given I'm on the catalog search page
  When I search for "BDD with Cucumber"
  Then I should see "Lawrence and Rayner" in the results

Scenario: Search for "cucumber"
  Given I'm on the catalog search page
  When I search for "cucumber"
  Then I should see "Cool as a Cucumber" in the results

Scenario: Search for "gherkin"
  Given I'm on the catalog search page
  When I search for "gherkin"
  Then I should see "Origami City: Fold More than 30 Global Landmarks" in the
  ➡ results
```

Combining the three scenarios into a scenario outline makes the repeated structure and variations in data more clear:

```
Scenario Outline: Search
  Given I'm on the catalog search page
  When I search for "<query>"
  Then I should see "<expected result>" in the results

  Examples:
    | query            | expected result                                 |
    | BDD with Cucumber | Lawrence and Rayner                            |
    | cucumber         | Cool as a Cucumber                              |
    | gherkin          | Origami City: Fold More than 30 Global Landmarks |
```

For each body row in the examples table, Cucumber replaces the placeholder values in the scenario outline (that is, `<query>`) with the corresponding values from the table before executing the scenario normally. (No change to the matching step definition is required.)

A scenario outline can be followed by multiple example tables, and tables can have a title. This can be a useful way to group examples and highlight important differences in data.

Use caution with scenario outlines, however. We recommend using them only when you have multiple regular, concrete scenarios that reveal a pattern. Programmers often reach for scenario outlines too early and end up creating features that are unreadable by nonprogrammers. In fact, most scenario outlines we've seen in the wild really shouldn't exist—concrete scenarios would be much more expressive.

Summary

- Separate the discovery step of BDD from the formalization and automation steps. Discovery is divergent and exploratory. Formalization is convergent.

- It's often best to formalize a first draft of a scenario with just a couple people and review it with a larger group than to try to write scenarios as a large group.

- In the Agile Testing Quadrants, BDD is a Quadrant 2 activity, producing business-facing tests that support development.

- BDD is complementary to manual, exploratory testing (which fits in Quadrant 3). It doesn't completely replace manual testing.

- Features and scenarios are formalized using Cucumber's Gherkin language.

- BDD is iterative, not linear. Don't try to do all the discovery, then all the formalization, then all the automation. Instead, identify some key examples, formalize a few of them, begin automating and implementing them, and then repeat as necessary to complete a user story.

Resources

Crispin, Lisa, and Janet Gregory. *Agile Testing: A Practical Guide for Testers and Agile Teams*. Hoboken: Pearson Education, Inc., 2009.

Hellesoy Aslak, "The World's Most Misunderstood Collaboration Tool": https://cucumber.io/blog/2014/03/03/the-worlds-most-misunderstood-collaboration-tool

Chapter 4

Automating Examples

Once we have a few examples specified as Cucumber scenarios in Gherkin, we're ready to turn them into automated tests to support the development of the new behavior we want.

In this chapter, we see what it looks like as the library team begins to automate their Cucumber scenarios, we consider the options for how to drive an application from Cucumber, and we look at how UI design fits into BDD.

Pairing On the First Step Definitions

Setting: RAJ's desk, in the team area.

(RAJ is looking at the feature file in a text editor on his screen, as JONAH pulls up a chair and joins him.)

JONAH: Hi, Raj. All ready to go?

RAJ: I think so. I checked the feature file into Git and pushed it and I've got it up here in my text editor. And I installed the Cucumber gem and ran it to make sure it's working.

JONAH: Great. How would you like to proceed?

RAJ: Can you remind me again, Jonah, how this stuff fits together? Jane and I have written browser automation using Selenium before, and we had some success with that. However, that was with me writing the automation code directly, not with a feature file. I remember we need step definition methods and that is where the automation code goes, but I'm struggling with how it fits into the whole testing stack.

JONAH: How about I draw you a picture and we walk through it? *(Pulls out a notebook and pen)*

RAJ: Yes, of course. That would be helpful.

JONAH: *(Drawing)* Here's the testing stack, at least for a web application like yours. First you have the Cucumber features, then underneath those are the Cucumber step definitions, which we are going to be writing soon. We won't likely have the next layer at this point, which consists of test helper methods, but I expect we'll refactor to that at some point this sprint. So, let's just assume it's there, since it's the more common case and what I usually recommend.

The step definition methods and/or test helper methods then call the web automation framework. This could be Selenium in Ruby, Java, or .NET. Many Ruby teams combine Selenium with the wrapper library Capybara to get nicer syntax. Or maybe they use WatiR instead of Selenium. Basically, it doesn't matter too much, it's mostly a question of what your team is comfortable using.

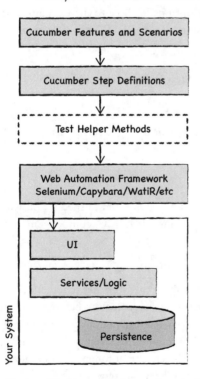

Figure 4-1 *The Cucumber stack with all automation through the UI*

RAJ: As you know, we're primarily a Ruby team. After the last round of automation, I did a lot of reading about Capybara and experimented with it a little. I like the level of abstraction Capybara provides over the top of Selenium in Ruby, so that's what I want to try with you.

JONAH: Sounds good. *(Circles Capybara in diagram.)* Everything from here down is likely to be similar to what you did last time. The web automation framework, Capybara in your case, calls down to the web UI, which calls your application, usually some kind of business objects layer sitting on top of a database.

The step definitions or helper methods can also call web services or some kind of API, so I'll draw that in here, but let's not worry about that for now. And, if you were automating something in-process it would, of course, look different from this.

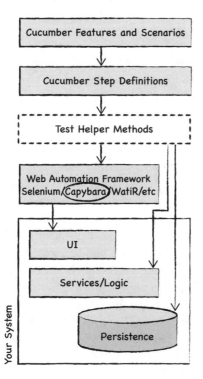

Figure 4-2 *Automation can drive the application below the UI when appropriate*

> So this is a common stack for Cucumber, at least with web apps. The main difference for us today is the top two or three layers.
>
> *RAJ*: OK, I see.
>
> Actually, what we'll be automating today won't have business objects or a database, since we'll be calling into the new search framework API to get the catalog search results back. So far, we've done a little of the top layer.
>
> *JONAH*: Yes, just one scenario, our happy path one. A very small, but meaningful, slice. Now we're going to follow that slice down through the stack.

The Test Automation Stack

Many people associate Cucumber with automated tests that drive a web user interface (UI), to the point where we've heard people say things like, "I can't use Cucumber because my project isn't a web app." As Jonah pointed out in the previous dialogue, you can drive a web UI from Cucumber but you're not actually using Cucumber to do it; you're using Capybara or Selenium or some other web driver library. Cucumber's step definitions are just the container for whatever code you use to drive your application, the glue between your scenarios and your automation.

Because Cucumber is used to describe a user's expectations about the behavior of an application, it's common to think about that behavior as the user would experience it—through the UI. And it's a small step to automate it the same way, opening web pages, filling out forms, and clicking links. However, Cucumber can be used to drive all kinds of applications. Moreover, many teams building web applications choose to have some or all of their step definitions drive the app below the UI.

We've coached teams who use Cucumber for command-line applications (like the Cucumber team does for Cucumber itself), mobile and desktop applications, even embedded software. In many cases, there are free, open-source utilities that help you drive your application, as Capybara does for web UIs. In other cases, you'll write custom helper code.

When working with Cucumber, you'll create two kinds of files: Feature files are where you put your scenarios and are written in the Gherkin language described in Chapter 3, "Formalizing Examples into Scenarios." Step definition files are where you put the code you want Cucumber to execute when it encounters a particular step.

Step definitions are code written in a general-purpose programming language like Ruby, Java, C#, or JavaScript.

Within each step definition, you'll write custom code to automate your application in various ways. For a web app, you'll load pages, click links, and fill out forms. For a command-line app, you'll execute a program and read stdout. It's common to use helper libraries like Selenium, Capybara, or Aruba for the actual automation—there's no need for each team to solve these common problems like loading a page in a web browser on their own.

In his book *Succeeding with Agile*, Mike Cohn introduces the concept of the test automation pyramid (see Figure 4-3). Simply put, it's the idea that most of your automated tests shouldn't go through the UI because automated UI tests are often slow and brittle. Instead, most tests should go below the UI, testing services or components below the UI or small units of code like classes and methods.

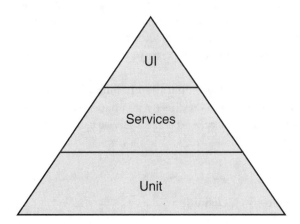

Figure 4-3 *The test automation pyramid*

This good advice has led to the following flawed logic: "Cucumber is the tool for UI tests. We shouldn't do many UI tests. Therefore, most of our tests should be in a unit test tool rather than in Cucumber." But this is mixing up two different concerns, the level of your architecture driven by the automated tests and the audience for the tests.

Cucumber is designed for customer-facing tests, for tests where you're describing customer expectations and want to use their language. Unit test tools like RSpec or JUnit are for developer-facing tests, where you're describing developer expectations. Either tool can be used to drive any layer of your application.

Many applications have significant business logic that doesn't live in the UI. Business stakeholders are naturally interested in the behavior of this business logic, so it's appropriate to describe the behavior with Cucumber scenarios. While the user will ultimately get at this behavior via the UI, the scenarios don't have to. They could skip the UI and drive the service or component directly. This will produce faster, easier-to-maintain tests.

For example, consider the logic for calculating fines and fees for overdue library books. Automating this through the UI would not only be slow, it would include significant amounts of the application incidental to the fine calculation. We'd have to check out books to a patron in various circumstances and simulate time passing just to set up the fine calculation. Our scenarios would be faster and more focused if they tested the fine calculation in isolation through a service interface or by directly using a fine calculator class.

Of course, this assumes that your business logic is decoupled from your UI. Teams adopting BDD for a legacy application thus find themselves with a chicken-and-egg problem. They want to refactor their application to make it more testable, but they can't refactor safely without good automated test coverage. In this case, treat the test pyramid as a goal rather than a starting point. Drive the application through the UI to build a safety net for refactoring. Refactor the application to get the business logic out of the UI. Then, refactor the tests to drive the application below the UI layer.

Most teams using Cucumber well drive their application in multiple ways, even within the same scenario. They might set up data directly in a database in a Given step, take an action through the UI in a When step, and make a service call to examine the state of the system in a Then step.

Creating Step Definitions

JONAH: How about you do the typing, and we'll work through this first scenario using the standard Cucumber loop of creating a pending step definition for each step, and then getting it to pass before moving on to the next one?

Let's start by running Cucumber against our feature file. Just type cucumber on the command line to get us going.

RAJ: Don't we need to pass it some parameters or something?

JONAH: Let's just go with the defaults for now. Since you put the feature file in the standard place, it'll know where to find it and just work.

RAJ: OK. *(Types command)* It found the feature file…

```
$ cucumber
Feature: Search for an ebook by title
  Library patron searches library catalog for a specific ebook
  so she can read it on her Kindle

  * Assume the library has the book in our catalog
  * Kindle books are Mobi format

  Scenario: Find an ebook for my Kindle by the exact title
    When I search ebooks for "Words of Radiance"
    Then I should see the following book at the top of my search results:
      | Name        | Words of Radiance |
      | Author      | Brandon Sanderson |
      | Call Number | FIC SANDERSO B    |
      | Format      | Kindle            |

1 scenario (1 undefined)
2 steps (2 undefined)
0m0.019s

You can implement step definitions for undefined steps with these snippets:

When("I search ebooks for {string}") do |string|
  pending # Write code here that turns the phrase above into concrete actions
end

Then("I should see the following book at the top of my search results:") do
➥ |table|
  # table is a Cucumber::MultilineArgument::DataTable
  pending # Write code here that turns the phrase above into concrete actions
end
```

What's that? Did it just print out the step definition for us in the console?

JONAH: Part of it. Let's copy that code into a new file and save it. We'll use it as the basis for our step definition methods. It doesn't matter whether you use Cucumber, Cucumber-JVM, or SpecFlow, they all work this way, generating step definition methods from your feature file steps to give you a head start.

RAJ: OK. *(Copies code)* What do I call it and where should I save it? Does it matter?

JONAH: Once again, it's convention-based, but let's not worry so much about the name at this point and just get it working. It will be easy enough to rename later once we figure it out. Just put it in the stepdef folder and call it whatever you like for now.

RAJ: OK. Done.

JONAH: Looks good. Now run Cucumber again and see what it does.

RAJ: Ah, the steps all show pending now.

```
$ cucumber
Feature: Search for an ebook by title
  Library patron searches library catalog for a specific ebook
  so she can read it on her Kindle

  * Assume the library has the book in our catalog
  * Kindle books are Mobi format

  Scenario: Find an ebook for my Kindle by the exact title
    When I search ebooks for "Words of Radiance"
      TODO (Cucumber::Pending)
      ./features/step_definitions/search_steps.rb:2:in '"I search ebooks
      ➥ for {string}"'
      features/ebook_search.feature:8:in 'When I search ebooks for
      ➥ "Words of Radiance"'

    Then I should see the following book at the top of my search results:
      | Name        | Words of Radiance |
      | Author      | Brandon Sanderson |
      | Call Number | FIC SANDERSO B    |
      | Format      | Kindle            |

1 scenario (1 pending)
2 steps (1 skipped, 1 pending)
0m0.011s
```

JONAH: Right. So now we can start implementing the steps. Let's start with the first one and fill in some pseudo code as comments.

RAJ: OK. We're trying to do two things in this step. *(Typing)*

```
# go to the ebook search page
# actually perform the search
```

JONAH: Do you know what the URL will be for the ebook search page?

RAJ: Not right now. Probably */ebooks*, I expect.

JONAH: OK, let's assume that */ebooks* is right for now. It's easy enough to change later. Replace that first comment with something like *(Writes on paper)*:

```
visit '/ebooks'
```

RAJ: OK. *(Typing)* Easy enough. I also need to add the Capybara gem to the Gemfile and get it installed. OK, done.

JONAH: Now run Cucumber again. `When I search ebooks for "Words of Radiance"` should now be a failing step.

RAJ: Yes, it is. It says "failing" instead of "pending," and it's red now instead of yellow.

JONAH: Great! We're making progress. Now we know the testing stack works, and we have an initial step that's failing. This is the "Red" step in the "Red, Green, Refactor" loop.

RAJ: You mean "Red" for failing test, "Green" for passing test, and "Refactor" for improving the underlying design without changing the behavior?

JONAH: Exactly. We're working test-first.

RAJ: So, should we get the step to green now?

JONAH: Almost, but we still need to replace that second comment. Our step fails now, but not quite for the right reason. We don't want to start making it pass until it actually does what it says.

RAJ: It seems odd that we're automating something that doesn't exist yet.

JONAH: I must admit, it's a big mindset shift. It was hard for me at the start too. It took me a long time before I got used to it—it really came with lots of practice. The way I learned to write code was: code, then test. BDD turns that on its head and says, "Let's specify what I'm going to build, using tests, then code it to make the tests pass."

I had to invest time in practicing working test-first until I became comfortable coding that way. Like any skill, it always feels awkward at first. I expect it will be the same for you and Robin, too.

RAJ: OK, understood. I'm not used to feeling like a beginner when I code. It will be good when that feeling passes.

JONAH: Absolutely. That's why I'm here, though. To help you through some of that awkward initial stage we all go through when we are learning a new skill.

Adjusting to Working Test-First

The first time you write a test that automates something that doesn't even exist yet can be jarring. Of course, time and practice help make working test-first feel more natural, but you can accelerate that process by reframing how you think about your tests.

Think of creating and automating scenarios as a design activity. You're expressing how you (and your customer) want the application to behave. You're saying, "I wish we could search for ebooks," or, "I wish the search results included a list of books with title, author, and call number." Then you run the tests to prove that things aren't as you wish, and you change the system to make it so.

Incorporating Mockups

RAJ: OK, what should I do now?

JONAH: One thing that can really help at this point is a UI mockup to guide our coding so we can write the automation code that actually tries to search. Do you normally create them?

RAJ: Sometimes. Robin and I have sketched out designs on our whiteboard in the past for very simple things, then we generally get Jessie to help us improve them. Jessie has a strong UXD background. In fact, that was her specialty before she took over as our ScrumMaster, so she generally takes care of any user experience design tasks for us.

JONAH: Great. How about we ask Jessie to help us out with this?

RAJ: Good idea.

(*Stands up and looks across the cube wall*) Excuse me, Jessie, do you have a few minutes to help us with some UI work?

JESSIE: Of course. What do you need?

JONAH: Nothing too fancy at this point, just a rough mockup of what the new ebook search results page might look like.

JESSIE: No problem. That will only take a few minutes to put together. I'll email it to you.

JONAH: Actually, Jessie. I was hoping you could just join us for a few minutes and we could work on it together, before you formalize it too much.

JESSIE: OK, let me come around to your side. (*Walks around*)

RAJ: Thank you.

(JESSIE pulls up a chair to RAJ's desk between RAJ and JONAH.)

JONAH: Great. Thanks, Jessie. For now, let's quickly sketch a draft together, agreeing on the HTML element IDs. Then Raj and I will have enough information to do a first pass at implementing the step definitions for the first scenario in the feature file.

JESSIE: I'm thinking the layout should be quite straightforward because it should match what we have now, with some minor improvements.

JONAH: I'd recommend we keep the language as consistent as possible between the scenario steps, what gets displayed in the UI, and the way we name things in the HTML.

JESSIE: Sure. *(Sketching on RAJ's notepad)* How about this?

JONAH: That looks good.

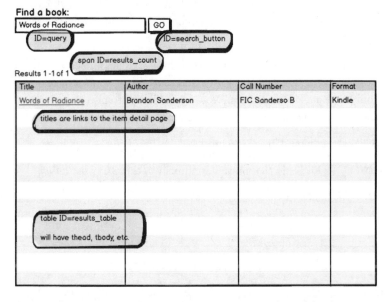

Figure 4-4 *An annotated UI mockup to support test-first UI development*

RAJ: So you're proposing that for the search form we have "query" and "search_button" as the elements, and then "Name," "Author," "Call Number," and "Format" as the search result elements in table rows, inside a table element called "results_table."

JESSIE: Yes, I considered doing it as an ordered list, but a table is more consistent with what we do today. Sound OK?

RAJ: Yes.

JONAH: Looks good to me. It would be good to work with this for now, as our initial approach, and get feedback from the rest of the team before we get too far into it or call it done. These kinds of things are easy to change at this point.

RAJ: Agreed. I like that we're having this conversation now. I would not want to go back and change a lot of markup later, if we can avoid it. What you said about keeping the language consistent wherever we can makes a lot of sense. It will help a lot. It's certainly not that way at the moment, which is one of the reasons it's very hard to make changes easily.

JESSIE: Yeah, much of the markup for our current website is very inconsistent and hard to work with.

JONAH: Well, hopefully we can start changing that, which will make your lives easier. Jessie, thanks so much for the good questions and the help on the UI.

JESSIE: No problem. I'll take a photo of these sketches and create mockups and flows for the other scenarios and send them around for review. It'll only take me a few minutes. Would you like me to also put together the new style sheet elements for you to use?

RAJ: Yes, that would be very helpful.

JESSIE: OK, I'll go do that now. Have fun. *(Walks back to her cube)*

JONAH: Thanks, Jessie.

Annotating Element Names in Mockups

In our BDD workshops, participants are often surprised that we'd advocate automating scenarios against a UI that doesn't exist yet. "Surely, we need to create the UI and then start writing the scenario." But we want the desired behavior to inform the UI design, so we like to lead with the scenarios. To give the developer something to automate against and to prevent the automation code from having to change too much, we like to use an annotated UI sketch or mockup.

The annotated mockup functions as the contract between step definitions that drive a UI and the UI itself. A minimal contract enables developers and designers to do most of their work in parallel. Precision here lets the UI designer continue to experiment and evolve the interface without breaking the scenarios. Developers can automate scenarios even against a UI that doesn't yet exist, while having confidence they won't need to redo their automation code when the actual UI gets implemented.

How Does User Experience Design Fit In to This?

BDD doesn't have anything to say about user experience design. This might lead some people to think that they shouldn't be doing any user experience design (UXD) at all if they are doing BDD. They might say, "I thought we are supposed to keep prototyping and mockups separate from doing BDD, or not do them at all."

In our experience, applying UXD will make a big difference to the success of BDD. UXD is the visual component of the same example-driven approach and is a wonderful complement to BDD. Because "a picture is worth a thousand words," applying UXD techniques better communicates what the software needs to do.

How do you decide where to start when exploring examples as you play the BDD game? Most people are visual thinkers, so it might be harder for them to follow along with purely text-based business examples or a formal "Given-When-Then" syntax. When walking through examples, we often find that a quick sketch can help illuminate what is needed.

We rarely talk through examples without drawing something on some kind of visible surface, such as a whiteboard or flip chart. We'll also often start with a mockup and use that to direct and guide the conversation about how the feature needs to work, especially for a new feature in an existing system or a feature that involves a lot of user interaction.

There's a virtuous cycle between creating mockups and distilling business examples. By "virtuous cycle" we mean that UXD and BDD reinforce each other in ways that are greater than just the sum of the parts. With BDD we seek out the business examples and business language that help us understand what the system needs to do, and with UXD we use those same examples and the same language to create diagrams and walkthroughs to further drive our understanding.

What we learn from the UXD conversations and artifacts such as UI mockups feeds back into Cucumber features and scenarios. Often, walking through draft screen designs and user flows leads to important discoveries about how the feature ought to work. We find that the more specific we are with the examples used in the user interaction conversations and diagrams, the better everyone understands what the user is trying to accomplish and why.

Of course, it's not always necessary to start with UXD. When the UI will be fairly straightforward or minimal, rather than do mockups of screens we typically find it's better to start with the business example and then plug in the UI discussion once we've got the examples clear. Or if the real domain complexity is in the business rules rather than in the UI, we almost always start with the business examples and seek to drive out a domain model that helps us make the complexity of the business domain more manageable.

Using Scenario Steps to Drive the Actual Implementation

RAJ: OK, what now?

JONAH: Simple. We've got Capybara installed and we've got our first step implemented. Let's run Cucumber again and see what happens.

RAJ: It worked. The browser came up and tried to take us to /ebooks on the library site, which is what should happen. It's a 404, but that is what we were expecting.

JONAH: Right. We're going to use these steps to drive the actual implementation. Normally, I would do this step by step, switching between writing the automation code and then implementing it.

RAJ: This page will take only a second to create. Give me a moment to wire up the route, view, and controller action. *(Typing)*

OK, done.

JONAH: Let's rerun Cucumber and see what we get.

RAJ: Nice. The browser came up as expected and now that step is green. Looks like we are moving forward.

JONAH: Right. It's a good start. Now we know our "plumbing" is working and we have the first step green to prove it.

That was the easy one. How good are you at the Capybara syntax?

RAJ: Still a beginner, but I have a quick reference here. So, we need to implement the search step now? Get it to put in the value and click the search button?

JONAH: Yes. We need to fill in the query, which in Capybara will be a `fill_in` method, with the value from the `query` argument that's coming in from the scenario. And then, just tell Capybara to click the search button, which will be a call to Capybara's `click_button` method.

RAJ: OK, I see. So it should look like this:

```
When("I search ebooks for {string}") do |query|
  visit '/ebooks'
  fill_in 'query', with: query
  click_button 'search_button'
end
```

JONAH: Right. If you run Cucumber again you'll see the search step fails.

RAJ: Yes, it fails. Shall we put a form in place?

JONAH: That's what I would do. So how about you create a simple form with those fields?

RAJ: OK, give me a few minutes here.

JONAH: No problem.

RAJ: The form is done. Now when I rerun Cucumber the first two steps are passing.

JONAH: Excellent. This last step will be the most involved, since we have quite a bit to verify. Plus, we're reading from a table argument on a step, which is different from what we've done so far.

Jessie's mockup shows the search results in a table, so we'll want to grab the first body row and assert on the data it contains.

RAJ: Something like this?

```
Then("I should see the following book at the top of my search results:")
➥ do |table|
  top_result = find('table#results_table tbody').first('tr')
end
```

JONAH: Yes, that's a great start. Let's add a line in there that checks that `top_result` actually has a value.

RAJ: OK, so we can do this:

```
Then("I should see the following book at the top of my search results:")
➥ do |table|
  top_result = find('table#results_table tbody').first('tr')
  expect(top_result).not_to be_nil,
  "Expected search results but didn't get any."
end
```

JONAH: Right. Let's try running that and see what we get.

RAJ: We got red for that step, and the error message, because we don't have any list items yet.

JONAH: Exactly. Now let's add the actual verification code after the `nil` check. How about we just check for title first, then get the others to work?

RAJ: OK.

JONAH: It should look something like this:

```
expected_book = table.rows_hash

actual_book = {}
actual_book['Title'] = top_result.find ('span.title').visible_text

expect(actual_book['Title']).to eq(expected_book ['Title'])
```

RAJ: Got it. And that one fails.

JONAH: Looks good, though. How about you hard code the result for now and see if we can get it to pass?

RAJ: You mean add some code to the view to display the title? That would be simple enough.

JONAH: Good idea.

RAJ: Alright! It passes. I know it's hard-coded, but it's good to finally see green.

JONAH: Totally. Let's just copy-paste the other book attributes for now and get it to work. We'll make some assumptions about what the

HTML element names will be, and then check those with Jessie to make sure we're on the same page.

RAJ: That's a lot of copy-paste.

```
Then("I should see the following book at the top of my search results:")
➥ do |table|

  top_result = find('table#results_table tbody').first('tr')
  expect(top_result).not_to be_nil,
     "Expected search results but didn't get any."

  actual_book = {}
  actual_book['Title'] = top_result.find('span.title').visible_text
  actual_book['Author'] = top_result.find('span.author').visible_text
  actual_book['Call Number'] = top_result.find('span.call_number').
                                 visible_text
  actual_book['Format'] = top_result.find('span.format').visible_text

  expected_book = table.rows_hash
  expect(actual_book['Title']).to eq(expected_book['Title'])
  expect(actual_book['Author']).to eq(expected_book['Author'])
  expect(actual_book['Call Number']).to \
    eq(expected_book['Call Number'])
  expect(actual_book['Format']).to eq(expected_book['Format'])
end
```

JONAH: Yes, for now. There are better ways to do this using Cucumber table objects, but let's go with this for now. We'll get it to work in terms of what is being displayed on the screen, then refactor it.

Did They Really Just Hard Code Those Results?

One of the surprising things for people new to working test-first is how small the steps are. Most developers faced with this scenario would have implemented the real search API call to make that Then step pass. But a single scenario searching for a single book really hasn't earned a full search implementation yet.

It's common in BDD (and TDD) to hard code the results to pass the first scenario. Then, the next scenario or two starts earning you variables. These small steps keep the system in a safe, working, comprehensible state at all times.

We can be confident that the first scenario tests what we think it tests. Sometimes, to increase that confidence, we'll play with the hard-coded implementation to ensure the scenario fails the way we expect it to. Change a letter in the book title, and the scenario should fail with a message about how the title doesn't match. Likewise for the other book attributes.

Now we can duplicate that scenario, change some of the data, and safely begin to grow a more realistic implementation.

Anatomy of a Step Definition

Step definitions are the link between your scenarios and the application they describe. They're the way you say to Cucumber, "When you come across a step in a scenario that sounds like this, here's the code I want you to execute."

All the different versions of Cucumber use Gherkin as the specification language, but each of them uses a different general-purpose programming language for step definitions. We saw the library team writing step definitions in Ruby. You could just as easily use Java, JavaScript, C#, or one of the many other supported languages.

The first step definition we saw connected this step:

```
When I search ebooks for "Words of Radiance"
```

to this bit of Ruby code:

```
When("I search ebooks for {string}") do |query|
  visit '/ebooks'
  fill_in 'query', with: query
  click_button 'search_button'
end
```

You might have expected the first line of the step definition to look something like this instead:

```
When('I search ebooks for "Words of Radiance"') do
```

But rather than simply matching the exact words of the step to the exact words of the step definition, Cucumber uses a special text matching language to connect the two. So, we don't need a new step definition for every title we want to search. Instead, we can make the search query a variable that gets passed from Gherkin into Ruby.

For many years, Cucumber used regular expressions to do this job of connecting steps and step definitions. Regular expressions can be intimidating. They have a reputation for being hard to use—so much so that it's become common in the programming world to quote Jamie Zawinski's quip, "Some people, when confronted with a problem, think *I know, I'll use regular expressions.* Now they have two problems."[1]

---

1. http://regex.info/blog/2006-09-15/247

As much as some of us like regular expressions, using them to identify step definitions is a bit like cutting birthday cake with a chainsaw—they're perhaps *too* powerful a tool. So, in 2017, Cucumber got its own text matching language, Cucumber Expressions. Cucumber Expressions still use regular expressions under the hood, but they enable you to handle simple cases without regular expressions and keep step definitions more readable in those cases where you do need a regular expression.

At the time of this writing, Cucumber Expressions are the default for the current Ruby, Java, and JavaScript versions of Cucumber. The generated snippets in those languages use Cucumber Expressions rather than regular expressions. SpecFlow, the .NET version of Cucumber, doesn't yet support Cucumber Expressions, so .NET developers will still need to use regular expressions directly.

Let's look at the simple Cucumber Expressions first, and then we'll explore the most useful parts of regular expressions and show how the two work together.

Simple Cucumber Expressions

Earlier, we saw the following step definition:

```
When("I search ebooks for {string}") do |query|
  visit '/ebooks'
  fill_in 'query', with: query
  click_button 'search_button'
end
```

which matched this step:

```
When I search ebooks for "Words of Radiance"
```

In the Cucumber Expressions language, {string} matches a string in quotes, captures the contents of the quotes, and discards the quotes. So, that same step definition would match steps like

```
When I search ebooks for "East of Eden"
```

and

```
When I search ebooks for "How to Open Locks with Improvised Tools"
```

but not

```
When I search ebooks for A Tale of Two Cities
```

because the latter has no quotes.

There are three other built-in types. {word} matches a single word. {int} matches positive and negative integers. {float} matches floating-point numbers. When you need to do anything beyond these four simple matches, you'll need to make your own custom Cucumber Expressions parameter type. And this requires regular expressions.

Regular Expressions

Regular expressions are the key to Cucumber's flexibility. Well-crafted regular expressions let you reuse step definitions, avoiding duplication and keeping your tests maintainable. But even experienced developers find them mysterious and overwhelming.

Fortunately, you don't need regular expressions like this one[2] to wield the power of Cucumber:

```
(?:[a-z0-9!#$%&'*+/=?^_`{|}~-]+(?:.[a-z0-9!#$%&'*+/=?^_`{|}~-]+)*|"
(?:[x01-x08x0bx0cx0e-x1fx21x23-x5bx5d-x7f]|[x01-x09x0bx0cx0e-x7f])*")
@(?:(?:[a-z0-9](?:[a-z0-9-]*[a-z0-9])?.)+[a-z0-9](?:[a-z0-9-]*[a-z0-9])?
|[(?:(?:25[0-5]|2[0-4][0-9]|[01]?[0-9][0-9]?).){3}(?:25[0-5]|2[0-4][0-9]|
[01]?[0-9][0-9]?|[a-z0-9-]*[a-z0-9]:(?:[x01-x08x0bx0cx0e-x1fx21-x5ax53-x7f]|
[x01-x09x0bx0cx0e-x7f])+)])
```

In fact, if you use regular expressions like this in your step definitions, you've gone too far. As with most things, the 80/20 rule applies. Only a handful of common, useful regular expression patterns are sufficient to make you a Cucumber power user.

> **Note**
> In this section, we assume you're using regular expressions directly for your step definitions. Then, in the next section, we show you how to use regular expressions to create custom Cucumber Expressions types.

Anchors

The regular expression I'm logged in matches I'm logged in and I'm logged in as an admin. To avoid ambiguous matches, use ^I'm logged in$.

---

2. This one matches almost any legal email address per the official specification. You should never have to do anything like this in a real Cucumber step definition.

The caret (^) at the beginning anchors to the beginning of the string. The dollar ($) at the end does the same with the end of the string. Use these with all your step definitions and you won't have surprise matches.

Wildcards and Quantifiers

Matching specific words is fine, but you often want flexibility to match a variety of strings. Table 4-1 shows some common patterns for non-exact matches.

Table 4-1 *Regular Expression Wildcards and Quantifiers*

Pattern	Matches
.*	Anything (or nothing), literally "any character (except a newline) 0 or more times"
.+	At least one of anything (except a newline)
[0-9]* or \d*	A series of digits (or nothing)
[0-9]+ or \d+	One or more digits
"[^\"]*" or ".*"	Something (or nothing) in double quotes
an?	A or an (the question mark makes the preceding item optional)

Capturing and Not Capturing

When you put part of a regular expression in parentheses, whatever it matches gets captured for use later. This is known as a *capture group*. In Cucumber, captured strings become step definition arguments. Typically, if you're using a wildcard, you probably want to capture the matching value for use in your step definition. If the When step earlier had used regular expressions instead of Cucumber Expressions, it would have looked like this:

```
When/^I search ebooks for "(.*)"$/ do |query|
  visit '/ebooks'
  fill_in 'query', with: query
  click_button 'search_button'
end
```

This step will work for virtually any search query, passing the matching query as an argument to the step definition.

Occasionally, you must use parentheses to get a regular expression to work, but you don't want to capture the match. For example, suppose we want to be able to match both When I log in as an admin and Given I'm logged in as an admin with the same step definition. After all, both step definitions do the same thing. There's no reason to have duplicated automation code in your step definitions simply because one is a `Given` step and one is a `When`.

We might write something like this:

```
When /^(I'm logged|I log) in as an? (.*)$/ do |role|
  # log in as the given role
end
```

The parentheses and pipe indicate a logical OR, just what we need to match two different strings.

This will fail to run, though. The regular expression captures two strings, but the step definition method takes only one. We need to designate the first group as non-capturing like this:

```
When /^(?:I'm logged|I log) in as an? (.*)$/ do |role|
  # log in as the given role
end
```

Now, with the addition of `?:` at the beginning of the group, it will perform as you expect.

> **Tip**
>
> You might be wondering how the attribute can be `When` and still match `Given I'm logged in as an admin`. It turns out that in Cucumber, it doesn't matter whether you use `Given`, `When`, or `Then` to define a step definition. They're all step definitions and are interchangeable. It's fairly common for today's `When` to be tomorrow's `Given`, as something moves from the feature under active development to a feature on which a new feature builds.

Just Enough

This is only the tip of the regular expression iceberg—whole books and websites are dedicated to the topic. But for day-to-day work with Cucumber, anchors, simple wildcards and quantifiers, and capturing and noncapturing groups are all you need.

Custom Cucumber Expressions Parameter Types

The built-in Cucumber Expressions types are a good starting point, but the real power of Cucumber Expressions is the capability to create and name your own types. For example, we often find it useful to have a few known test users with different roles and to identify them by their role name. To keep it simple for illustration purposes, let's suppose we have three: You can use the system as a librarian, a library patron, or an administrator and it should behave differently in each case. We'd like to encapsulate the details of the username and password in a single place in our step definition code.

The three steps we'd want to match are:

```
Given I'm a librarian
Given I'm a library patron
Given I'm an administrator
```

There's no built-in Cucumber Expressions type that can match all of these. We could, of course, create three separate step definitions, but because they're all doing the same thing with different users, it makes sense to have that sign-in logic in one place.

We'll define a custom parameter type like this:

```
ParameterType(
    name:         'role',
    regexp:       /an? (librarian|library patron|administrator)/,
    type:         UserCredentials,
    transformer: ->(role) {
      case role
      when "librarian"
        u = UserCredentials.new
        u.username = "sarah@publiclibrary.org"
        u.password = "7EUVZH^gJv6x"
        u
      when "library patron"
        u = UserCredentials.new
        u.username = "bob.ross@gmail.com"
        u.password = "DRf7Y,9ZBCVB"
        u
      when "administrator"
        u = UserCredentials.new
        u.username = "nina@publiclibrary.org"
        u.password = "67AdHrTDrNo."
        u
      end
    }
)
```

Now, our step definition doesn't have to know about the user types and their credentials; it will just receive a `UserCredentials` object populated with the appropriate values. Here's how it might look if we have a helper method we can call to navigate to the library home page and log in with the provided credentials:

```
Given "I'm {role}" do |role_credentials|
  helper.login_with(role_credentials.username, role_credentials.password)
end
```

This keeps our step definition code simple and expressive.

Because Cucumber Expressions use regular expressions under the covers, it's still important to understand how simple regular expressions work. But there's no longer a need to work with regular expressions as part of every step definition.

Beyond Ruby

We've seen that a step definition is simply a block of code identified by a step-matching regular expression. Each language version of Cucumber has its own way of associating code with regular expressions. In the previous dialogue, Raj created a step definition in Ruby that looked like this:

```
When("I search ebooks for {string}") do |query|
  visit '/ebooks'
  fill_in 'query', with: query
  click_button 'search_button'
end
```

Here's how the same step definition might look in Java:

```
@When("I search ebooks for {string}")
public void searchEbooksFor(String query) {
  // go to ebook search page
  // fill in the query text box
  // click the search button
}
```

In JavaScript:

```
When("I search ebooks for {string}", function(query) {
  // go to ebook search page
  // fill in the query text box
  // click the search button
})
```

And in C# (where we still need regular expressions because Cucumber Expressions aren't supported yet):

```
[When(@"I search ebooks for ""(.*)""")]
public void SearchEbooksFor(string query) {
  // go to ebook search page
  // fill in the query text box
  // click the search button
}
```

All four of these simply associate a Cucumber Expression or regular expression with a block of code in a way appropriate to each language.

Continuing to Implement the Scenario

RAJ: OK, I'm adding more hard coding to the controller for the other book attributes... *(Typing)*

Done. Now to run Cucumber, and all the steps are now passing, and the first scenario is now passing too.

JONAH: Good. Now we've at least verified that everything is wired up in terms of test automation. That's an important point to get to at this early stage. We're not finished, of course. What's still to be done?

RAJ: Let me see. There are still the remaining lower layers in your diagram to fill out, which is the actual application work. We don't have a domain layer in our case, since we are calling a Ruby library that wraps the search API. So we still need to *(Writing)*

1. Pass our search parameters to our search framework.

2. Wire up the controller to our search framework results so we are getting real data for the search results, and pass that data through to the view.

3. Do the actual page designs, including formatting the search results correctly.

4. Refactor the final step-definition code to use the table comparison logic you mentioned.

JONAH: That sounds right to me, too. Normally, I would probably be doing those sorts of full-stack things as I go through and implement the steps, but since we are doing this for the first time I thought it important we get a little momentum here at the start. As you say, they are still tasks that need to be finished for this first search story to be considered done.

RAJ: Is this where someone would use RSpec to drive out the actual implementation?

JONAH: Exactly. That's my typical approach: use RSpec or minitest, or whatever your favorite unit-testing framework is, to drive out test-first the API call to the search framework and the interactions between the model, view, and controller objects in your web framework.

Since you're not already doing TDD, though, I'd suggest waiting and learning just one new tool and practice at a time. Your Cucumber scenarios will give you coverage you can use later to retrofit unit tests safely. Plus, you'll see the value of small, fast unit tests as your library of slower scenarios grows. The two play nicely together, but it would be a lot to learn all at once.

RAJ: OK. I'm pretty comfortable with doing all the rest, and it shouldn't take me long. As you said before, since we already have *Words of Radiance* as a Kindle book in our catalog, it will come up as the first result from our new search framework, so our test will still pass and we won't have to do complicated data setup for this first story.

JONAH: Good.

I see Robin is back here. Hi, Robin. Did you, Sam, and Jane finish cleanup on the rest of the feature file scenarios?

ROBIN: Yes. They're as good as we can make them at this point. I've checked our updates into the repository, so you can pull them down.

RAJ: Thank you. Getting them now…

OK, so we have the complete feature file now.

JONAH: Right, for now, a least. Until you find some new scenarios.

JESSIE: *(Poking her head over the cube wall)* Raj, I've diagrammed out the UI mockups for this story, showing the variations by scenario. Since we want consistency with the HTML element names, I also went ahead and annotated them on the mockup. They should be what we agreed, and the mockups and flows should be straightforward enough for everyone, including Mark, to follow. Let me know if you have any questions. Oh, I also put them up on the team Wiki and emailed everyone on the team to get their feedback.

RAJ: Thanks, Jessie. I see it. It looks good, and the element names you've annotated are exactly what we agreed. This will be very helpful in getting the page designs completed and staying consistent with our markup.

Slowing Down to Speed Up

JONAH: Looks like there's enough here to finish this story now.

RAJ: Agreed. Thank you for your help, Jonah. As I said before, this way of working seems strange to me today, but what you are saying makes sense and I am hopeful I will become more comfortable with it. I just didn't realize it would be such a change.

We haven't made a lot of overall progress yet, but it's only the first day, and usually by this point we wouldn't have anything to show yet. We would have started a lot of things, but that would be all.

JONAH: I'm very encouraged and excited by the level of collaboration I am seeing so far. I get the impression it's unusual for your team to be working together on the same features in this way.

RAJ: Absolutely. Apart from Robin and me, we're quite siloed, especially from Jane. We also don't talk with Mark and Sam all that much, except in sprint planning. This seems more like a whole-team approach, even if we are getting a slow start. Normally by now I'd have the coding done. Is doing this the "BDD way" always going to take longer?

JONAH: Don't be too discouraged about a perceived lack of progress at this early stage. Sometimes you have to slow down a little to go faster, especially if the right direction is still a little unclear.

RAJ: OK, I understand, but I feel that even though I've learned a lot today, we haven't actually coded much yet.

JONAH: Don't forget, learning *is* progress. Creating working software is progress, even if it's incomplete. That's what incremental and iterative development is all about. You don't yet have a production-ready product increment, so it's not done by any means, but you *have* made significant progress so far.

RAJ: It doesn't feel that significant.

JONAH: Go easier on yourself and the team. It's only the first day and you've already coded up enough of the first scenario to demo what you've done so far and get feedback from Mark and the rest of the team. When you combine that with Jessie's mockups, that's progress.

And if you and Robin are able to wire up the actual search API this afternoon, you might even have every part of a vertical slice to demo, even if the UI still needs work to finish. But don't worry if you don't finish wiring it up today, since you already have enough of it done to show Mark and make sure we are on the right track.

RAJ: Good point. Yes, I'm looking forward to demoing this to Mark tomorrow morning.

JONAH: Me too.

Remember, it's important at this stage to focus on the positive things you are experiencing, especially as you get used to the new practices. It's easy to lose heart when learning new team skills and techniques and give up on them, without giving yourself enough time to grow into them. That's one reason why we paired on this first scenario, and why we focus on a high-value feature as early as we could while introducing as little technical friction as possible. This approach helps you overcome the inertia of getting started and build up some early speed while seeing early value.

RAJ: I see.

JONAH: Getting this first story done is mostly about building the right feature. Once you have that, the rest of the effort is in building the feature right.

RAJ: What do you mean, "building the right feature" versus "building the feature right?"

JONAH: I mean the biggest risk in software development is working on the wrong feature: delivering the wrong thing, something the customer doesn't want. It's the risk of delivering something that does not meet the customer need. BDD helps you build the right thing by using concrete business examples, by shortening the feedback loop with the product perspective that Mark brings, and by incorporating in an ongoing way the business process specification and feature verification perspectives that Sam and Jane bring to the effort.

> *RAJ*: OK, what do you mean by "getting the feature right" then?
>
> *JONAH*: Well, that's about the details of the implementation: how you actually code and deliver it. The sufficiency of the underlying design, the quality of the code and tests, the robustness of the infrastructure you deploy to, etc. Basically, it's about how good the technical solution is.
>
> *RAJ*: Understood. This is a lot to think about, especially when the automation tasks are added in too.
>
> *JONAH*: Absolutely. This is also why I sketched out the automation stack the way I did, so you could see it's not that different from what you have done in the past. The main difference BDD brings is the use of the feature file to capture, distill, and document the business examples.
>
> *RAJ*: I can see that. I will make sure to take a similar approach when I pair with Robin on the rest of the automation work.
>
> *JONAH*: Great! I'll leave you to it.

Slow Is Normal (at First)

Learning a new practice takes time. In a book, this is almost too obvious to say, but on an actual project, it's easy to forget; it's easy to become impatient and give up before you really get going.

To make space for learning when adopting a new practice, we recommended what we call the *slow lane* approach in Chapter 2, "Exploring with Examples." This becomes particularly important with the automation side of BDD for two reasons. First, automating your first few scenarios just takes a long time. It's a new skill using new tools, and the first scenarios take the cost of a lot of the basic setup and infrastructure. Second, your early automation usually isn't very good. It takes time to learn which patterns work in your context and which don't. It's better to learn this slowly, with a small number of scenarios, than to scale your automation before you learn how to do it well. For this reason, we encourage teams to still use the slow lane, even when everyone is enthusiastic about getting started.

Testing APIs

Setting: Raj's desk

JONAH: Those first couple scenarios are good. You're proving that ebook search works and you grew a nice UI for users to find the books they want.

Now, you mentioned that you have a search API you're calling from the website. Is that right?

RAJ: Yes, that's correct. Why do you ask?

JONAH: As you've come up with more variations of search to test, you really don't need them all to go through the UI. I'd recommend you have the steps for these other search scenarios exercise the search service API directly, rather than run out-of-process against the browser using Capybara. You could use a tag for the scenario, like `@api`, to indicate this.

ROBIN: That would be simple enough, but what does it gain us?

RAJ: I think I know. It would eliminate the added complexity and time of having to drive the browser and verify the component that contains the actual behavior under test: the API. Is that right?

JONAH: Yes, it is.

ROBIN: Makes sense. But shouldn't we just use RSpec for the API tests? Why put them in Cucumber?

JONAH: For me, adding this one as a Cucumber scenario is a better choice because it exposes the business rules as part of your living executable documentation via the feature file. Putting it in RSpec tends to make it more of a coding implementation concern that is hidden from the rest of the team.

Keep in mind that there's no hard and fast rule for which tool to use. Teams tend to develop their own guidelines.

You want to keep the number of full-stack automated tests to a minimum. They will tend to be brittle and slow. If you can push your testing down to a lower layer or component, then all the better. Your tests will be faster, more robust, and less likely to change unless the business rules change.

Using a tag in the feature file provides an elegant way to indicate that you are going against the API for this scenario rather than the entire stack. I would expect over time that you would find more and more API-level scenarios.

Definitely keep the first couple scenarios to prove search works end to end, but you don't need to go end to end for every search variation.

Choose Cucumber Based on Audience, Not Scope

A common misconception about Cucumber is that it's for tests that drive an application through the user interface. Teams often do drive their UI from Cucumber, but that's not why Cucumber is the right tool. Cucumber is the right tool when you want to expose system behavior to business stakeholders, regardless of the architectural layer at which the step definitions drive the application. Unit test tools like RSpec or JUnit are the right tools when the behavior only needs to be exposed to developers. Or to put it slightly differently: Cucumber is for testing customer intent, unit test tools are for testing developer intent. In Chapter 3, we introduced the Agile Testing Quadrants, which referred to these as Quadrant 2 and Quadrant 1 tests, respectively.

In the previous dialogue, the team had begun to accumulate more and more ebook search scenarios. Users obviously care about search, so it makes sense that the behavior would show up in Cucumber scenarios (Quadrant 2). Of course, they'll use it through the UI, but this doesn't require that every search scenario be automated through the UI. If the code in the UI is the same for any search, the team could drive the search API in isolation for most of the search scenarios.

To give the extreme case, Richard once worked on a team where it made sense to use BDD to drive the behavior of a single class. (This was before Cucumber had a viable .NET option, so we used a different tool, but we'd choose Cucumber today.) This application had complicated logic to determine the risk associated with a prospective apartment renter. It used the prospective renter's credit and rental history along with various other factors to produce recommendations about how risky the renter was, how much security deposit to collect, and the like.

Of course, this behavior would be exposed through a user interface. But when the team is trying to grow and prove the behavior of this tricky algorithm, going through the UI to create a new rental application added significant overhead to each scenario that really wouldn't help the team get the algorithm right. Instead, the team created a suite of scenarios around just the risk calculator class. They had a separate set of scenarios that went through the UI to prove that the risk calculations worked in context, but that context wasn't required for all the nuances in the algorithm. Ultimately, it comes down to creating the fastest automation we can that realistically exposes the system behavior to business stakeholders.

Summary

- Cucumber scenarios are automated by creating step definitions, bits of code that run for each step in a scenario.

- Step definitions are linked to steps using regular expressions or Cucumber Expressions, giving you reusability as data in steps changes.

- Step definitions are just containers for automation code. You create whatever code you need to put in that container, often using helper libraries like Selenium, Capybara, or Aruba.

- Choose the fastest, most realistic way of driving your application. Often this means driving the application though the UI, but it doesn't have to. Driving a service, an API, or even a database directly can be a better choice for a particular step.

- Use a Cucumber scenario to describe behavior whenever the user or customer cares about the behavior, regardless of the size of the thing being automated. A Cucumber scenario that calls a single class is OK.

Chapter 5

Frequent Delivery and Visibility

Most software teams spend most of their time in an "in-progress" state, with the product only partially working, punctuated by occasional moments of "done" when deadlines hit. Teams using BDD can be in a stable done state multiple times per day. This creates opportunities for earlier and more frequent feedback from testers, product managers, stakeholders, and customers.

In this chapter, we look at the many ways a team's behavior might change to take advantage of that more frequent delivery and increased visibility. We pay particular attention to how the tester's role changes in BDD.

How BDD Changes the Tester's Role

A good tester is a good questioner. What happens when the user starts from this context instead of that one? What might produce this outcome instead of that one?

Much of manual testing is asking the same questions over and over again. Testers shouldn't do this; computers can. Indeed, computers can do it better. They don't get bored or tired or distracted. If we can trust the computer to keep asking the questions we already know about, we can free the tester to ask new ones.

In BDD, testers bring this questioning to bear in two places: when the team is first exploring the behavior of new stories and when the known scenarios pass and it's time to discover new ones that ought to pass but don't yet. In the following dialogue, we see both. Jane has helped the team discover and refine the initial set of scenarios, and she explores the boundaries of the system's new behavior to find other scenarios that might be missing.

Refining the Scenarios and Exploring for New Ones

JANES's desk, in the team area.

(JANE is looking at the feature file in a text editor on her screen and testing the new search feature. JONAH comes over to her desk.)

JANE: Hi, Jonah. We all driving you crazy yet?

JONAH: Ha! No, not yet. How goes the testing?

JANE: Good. Raj and Robin did a good job of implementing the rest of the scenarios. Here's what the feature file looks like now:

```
Feature: Search for a Kindle ebook by title
  Library patron searches library catalog for a specific ebook
  so she can read it on her Kindle

  * Assume the library has the book in our catalog
  * Kindle books are Mobi format


  Scenario: Exact title
    When I search ebooks for "Words of Radiance"
    Then I should see the following book at the top of my search results:
      | Title       | Words of Radiance |
      | Author      | Brandon Sanderson |
      | Call Number | FIC SANDERSO B    |
      | Format      | Kindle            |

  Scenario: Important word in the title
    When I search ebooks for "Radiance"
    Then I should see the following book in my search results:
      | Title       | Words of Radiance |
      | Author      | Brandon Sanderson |
      | Call Number | FIC SANDERSO B    |
      | Format      | Kindle            |

  Scenario: No words from the title
    When I search ebooks for "Horses"
    Then I should not see the following book in my search results:
      | Title       | Words of Radiance |
      | Author      | Brandon Sanderson |
      | Call Number | FIC SANDERSO B    |
      | Format      | Kindle            |
```

```
Scenario: Book not in the catalog
  When I search ebooks for "Astronomicum Caesareum"
  Then I should see the following message:
    """
    Item not found in catalog
    """
```

JONAH: Excellent.

JANE: I've confirmed that the steps and step definitions line up with the mockups Jessie created in terms of layout, style, and the HTML elements. So, we are all good there. So far, I haven't found any bugs.

JONAH: Very glad to hear that.

JANE: As we grow more scenarios, though, I'm getting uncomfortable with just assuming we have and don't have certain items in the catalog. I'd prefer that the feature say something about the initial state of the catalog. That's what I'd do in my test cases.

JONAH: Choosing a book like *Words of Radiance* that was already in the catalog simplified automation, so I think that was a good call to get moving quickly. And you can stick with that decision while still making the initial state explicit in a `Given` step. In fact, I'll sometimes do `Given` steps that just check that the initial state is what you expect it to be. The step doesn't have to put the book in the catalog; it can just assert that the expected book is there.

JANE: So, do I just add a `Given` step to each scenario about the book? Like... `Given the catalog contains "Words of Radiance"`?

JONAH: Sure, let's start there.

JANE: *(Typing)* There we go.

JONAH: Now, what do you notice about the feature?

JANE: Well...obviously, I'm writing the same `Given` over and over again. It would be nice if I could clean that up.

JONAH: Yep. Remember that `Background` keyword we talked about in the Gherkin overview? This is where we use it. You can move those `Given`s up to a single `Given` in the `Background`. But before we do that, what else do you see when you look at a single scenario now?

JANE: Hmm. I notice that we talk about the book differently in the `Given` and `Then` steps. The `Given` just has the title, while the `Then` has other attributes. It looks kind of weird.

JONAH: Good catch. I like symmetry between `Givens` and `Thens` when I can get it, so I'd add the other attributes to the `Given`.

JANE: (Typing) Like this?

```
Scenario: Exact title
  Given the ebook catalog contains:
    | Title       | Words of Radiance |
    | Author      | Brandon Sanderson |
    | Call Number | FIC SANDERSO B    |
    | Format      | Kindle            |
  When I search ebooks for "Words of Radiance"
  Then I should see the following book at the top of my search results:
    | Title       | Words of Radiance |
    | Author      | Brandon Sanderson |
    | Call Number | FIC SANDERSO B    |
    | Format      | Kindle            |
```

JONAH: Yes. Now, let's extract those `Given` steps into a `Background` section.

JANE: (Typing) Here we go. And I'll delete that assumption about the book being in the catalog since we're making it an explicit precondition now.

I'll get the other `Given` about the book not being in the catalog in there, too. I'm not going to add attributes other than the book's title for now. I don't think anything else matters for a book not in the catalog.

What do you think of this?

```
Feature: Search for a Kindle ebook by title
  Library patron searches library catalog for a specific ebook
  so she can read it on her Kindle

  (Kindle books are Mobi format)


  Background:
    Given the ebook catalog contains:
      | Title       | Words of Radiance |
      | Author      | Brandon Sanderson |
      | Call Number | FIC SANDERSO B    |
      | Format      | Kindle            |
```

```
And the ebook catalog does not contain:
  | Title          | Astronomicum Caesareum |

Scenario: Exact title
  When I search ebooks for "Words of Radiance"
  Then I should see the following book at the top of my search results:
    | Title          | Words of Radiance |
    | Author         | Brandon Sanderson |
    | Call Number    | FIC SANDERSO B    |
    | Format         | Kindle            |
```

JONAH: I like it. There's just one small thing I'd change at this point.

The symmetry between the `Given` and `Then` steps is nice, but thinking ahead just a little bit, it makes sense for a catalog to have more than one book in it. And that suggests to me rotating the table to have a header row and a row for each book. It breaks the symmetry a little bit, but I think it'll make more sense to the reader and keep the automation from having to totally change when a second book is added. I try not to get ahead of myself too far, but this feels like an OK way to leave options for the future.

JANE: OK, so like this?

```
Background:
  Given the ebook catalog contains:
    | Title            | Author            | Call Number   | Format |
    | Words of Radiance | Brandon Sanderson | FIC SANDERSO B | Kindle |
  And the ebook catalog does not contain:
    | Title            |
    | Astronomicum Caesareum |
```

JONAH: Perfect.

JANE: Usually by this stage I'd be figuring out the test cases on my own, wondering what it was that Raj and Robin actually did. This way, I knew before they started coding what the feature would look like, so I know exactly what the feature functionality should be, and thus what "done" means for this first ebook search story.

Admittedly, it's a small feature with not much in the way of UI. But I realize there's a lot going on with the plumbing for the search, and together we all did a good job of capturing the test scenarios. It's made my work much easier.

JONAH: Has it? How so?

JANE: It's like I hoped. Raj showed me the Cucumber tests running, so I was able to verify that it's doing the right thing for the scenarios we laid out. We even paired on coding up the step definitions for the final scenario, so I have a good understanding of how that works too.

The test plan writing and simple manual testing I would normally spend a lot of time on was already finished prior to me looking at it.

Another good thing is that Raj and Robin had a couple of questions for me as they implemented the story. They wanted to know how I would be checking one of the scenarios from a testing perspective. My input was valued and useful instead of being the bad news that comes when everyone thinks they're done and it's too late to do anything about it.

JONAH: You mentioned Raj showed you the Cucumber scenarios passing. What about the test automation part of this BDD approach—how do you think that will change what you do going forward?

JANE: I'm usually pretty enthusiastic about trying things that can help me be more effective with my time, and so far this is a huge improvement for me. Since these are now automated tests, I've now got a small, but growing, set of regression tests around this key new functionality.

JONAH: Sure. Sounds like good progress for you.

JANE: Yes, it is. Now I can focus on exploratory testing, on trying to break the functionality now that I have it. I'm not spending time on so much monkey work like I used to, since I know we've got all the important acceptance tests covered.

Exploratory testing is where I would rather spend my time anyway, since you can't automate the kind of thinking and exploring I do to look for bugs in the application.

JONAH: We did find some edge cases in our team discussion though. How do those play into this?

JANE: The reality is in the past I would often find lots of those kinds of edge-case issues *after* some new functionality is implemented, rather than before. Sometimes they were things that I could not believe the developers missed.

It was great that we were able to catch and document some edge cases in our team discussions, because the ones we covered in the feature file were—in my mind, at least—central to how the feature should actually work. If we had not covered those, it would be hard for me to think of the feature as actually even working correctly.

JONAH: That's how I tend to think about this, too. I wonder, since exploratory testing is a real strength for you, if you end up being able to push even more test scenarios earlier in the process.

JANE: That would certainly be nice, and I'll do my best. I'm hoping to get better at identifying and highlighting those as we discuss examples for the feature files, but for now I'm just glad I've got more time to think about them instead of the basic cases I usually end up spending most of my time on.

JONAH: Did you find anything so far as you've been manually testing the new ebook search? Anything we missed as a team when we were discussing the examples?

JANE: Well, I've been thinking about the search terms we use: In the feature file we perhaps didn't cover quite as many combinations as we should, especially concerning how many of the keywords are in the title.

JONAH: What do you mean? Can you give me some examples?

JANE: Of course. For example, what about the following search terms? *(Writes on notepad)*

- radiant words

- radiance

- radiant

- words

How should those search terms be handled? It seems to me that the rule should be that every keyword should be in the title for the title to be found. I saw some inconsistencies.

JONAH: I think I know what you mean by that, but I could have it wrong.

JANE: I was actually just getting ready to enter this into our system as a bug report.

JONAH: Well, before you enter it in as a bug report, how about we get Raj and Robin to come over and discuss it with them? It certainly might be worth a bug report, but on the other hand it might be a small thing they could resolve quickly that might not warrant entering a bug, especially since the story isn't done yet.

To me, it's not really even possible to have a bug in an incomplete story—the story's just not done yet.

JANE: Good idea. I'd rather not enter a bug report if I don't need to. Raj, Robin, do you have time to discuss the new search story?

(RAJ and ROBIN come over to JANE's desk in the team area)

RAJ: Hi, Jane. Robin and I were just doing a little technical documentation of the search API while you did your testing. Nothing that would impact your work.

JANE: That's fine. Thanks for letting me know.

I was just talking with Jonah about how my testing has been going and mentioned to him I found some inconsistencies in the handling of certain search terms. I wrote them down here on my notepad.

RAJ: OK, I see. What is the concern?

JANE: Well, in these examples, it seemed to me the rule should be that every keyword should be in the title for the book to be found.

ROBIN: I don't understand what you mean. Are you saying these search terms should work, or not?

JONAH: How about we go through each example and see?

JANE: That's a good idea. So, this first one is "radiant words." It seems to me that since "radiant" is not in the book title, it should not return Words of Radiance in the search results.

JONAH: What about the other ones?

JANE: Let me mark each one based on whether I think it should match or not:

- radiant words—no
- radiance—yes
- radiant—no
- words—yes

RAJ: Ah, I see.

ROBIN: Me too. I get what you mean by the rule now. "Radiant" is not even a word in the book title, though it is close, so it wouldn't match to our book at all.

JANE: Yes, that's what I was saying. It seems to me we want to enforce a search that is much tighter than our current one, which seems to return just about anything close to what the user entered.

RAJ: Yes, it certainly does. I agree; it needs to be less inclusive in this way you have identified. More specific.

ROBIN: We can dial back the matching algorithm in the API, right Raj?

RAJ: Yes, this should be quite straightforward to implement.

JONAH: Jane was thinking of following your normal process of creating a bug report, but what if you just added a new scenario to the feature file for this first and then just followed the regular process?

RAJ: No problem, we can do that. Jane, do you have a few minutes to write up a new scenario in the feature file with us right now? We can do it at my desk, if you like.

JANE: Of course. It'll take about the same time it was going to take me to file a bug report anyway.

ROBIN: This might even be quicker. Plus, you get to hang with us more!

JANE: *(Laughs)* Well, that is true.

> *JONAH:* Sounds great. Is this something you should get Mark's opinion on first?
>
> *RAJ:* Yes, Mark is in his office. Jane, how about you and I go ask him right now? Though I'm confident he'll agree, it's worth checking by walking through the example with him.
>
> *JANE:* Sounds good. Let's check with Sam too on the way back.
>
> *(JANE and RAJ walk down the corridor to MARK's office.)*

Exploratory Testing

Rather than inspecting for quality late in development and filing bug reports, testers in BDD actively engage in helping the team build quality in from the beginning. They collaborate with product people and developers in identifying and specifying scenarios. They may participate in the automation of those scenarios. Sometimes, they'll even pair with developers as they make the scenarios pass so they gain an understanding of the implementation. Then, as scenarios begin to pass, testers do exploratory testing to identify missing scenarios. And the cycle continues.

Manual regression testing can take so much time that some testers are largely unfamiliar with exploratory testing. Elisabeth Hendrickson, author of the excellent book on the topic, *Explore It!*, describes exploratory testing as, "Simultaneously learning about the system while designing and executing tests, using feedback from the last test to inform the next."[1]

In an exploratory testing session, testers use their experience, intuition, and heuristics to try new scenarios around the edges of the system's current behavior. When they find something that doesn't work as expected, they note a possible missing scenario for discussion with other team members and use that insight to decide what to explore next.

This is unlike traditional manual testing in a few key ways. First, testers don't attempt to plan a whole set of test cases in advance. Instead, they use the outcome of each test to inform where to go next. Second, they don't waste time documenting everything that they test. If the system behaves correctly, they move on (unless they've identified a behavior that's not documented well in the current Cucumber scenarios). Finally, unexpected behaviors are used to drive collaboration and, ultimately, to help

---

1. https://pragprog.com/book/ehxta/explore-it

the team build the right thing today, rather than just documented as bug reports. Bug reports are reserved for documenting things the team called "done" that were, in fact, not done.

In the previous dialogue, the new behaviors Jane discovered in her exploratory testing were relatively small, so Raj and Robin were able to add them to the current user story. Sometimes, the new behaviors are large or not worth building right away. In those cases, the product owner might choose to create a new story further down the backlog or might simply choose to note the behaviors for potential inclusion later.

Integrating Cucumber into the Automated Build

RAJ and ROBIN are back at RAJ's desk.

> RAJ: OK, that's the last of the scenarios we needed to automate right now. Let me check this in.
>
> You know, we really should be running these scenarios as part of our continuous integration. Then, everybody could see where we stand.
>
> ROBIN: Yeah. Here, I'll pull up the configuration.
>
> Oh, look, there's already Cucumber support in TeamCity. Let's turn it on.
>
> RAJ: I like it. Kick off a build so we can see it run.
>
> ROBIN: *(Clicking)* Ooh, that's a nice report. I think Mark's gonna like this.
>
> *(JANE pokes her head around the corner)*
>
> JANE: Guys, do you know what happened to my test environment?
>
> RAJ: No, what do you mean?
>
> JANE: I was working through some more exploratory testing and the web server stopped responding for a moment, and then when I refreshed my browser, my test data was gone.
>
> ROBIN: Oh. Raj, we ran the Cucumber suite on the test environment.
>
> RAJ: And it resets the test database.
>
> We need another environment. I'll get the OK from Mark to have Brian set one up just for Cucumber.

> *ROBIN:* And I'll turn off Cucumber in the build for now. Sorry, Jane.
>
> *JANE:* That's OK. I'm glad we got it sorted out so quickly.

BDD and Automated Builds

The frequent feedback offered by BDD is more useful if it's shared by the team. Sometimes, we coach teams to adopt BDD who don't yet have an automated build system. BDD can help developers work incrementally. But it's much more valuable to have the full suite of scenarios running regularly in a visible environment so everyone can see the state of the system at all times. We recommend adopting automated builds, ideally continuous integration, alongside or shortly after BDD.

This implies a need for a dedicated environment. At one client, each team had a shared QA environment, used by testers for manual testing. They couldn't get access to another environment, so they simply repurposed the QA environment for running the Cucumber scenarios. It quickly became clear this was untenable. An automated build would kick off in the middle of a manual testing session, wiping out the tester's data and interrupting his or her work. Or, the team would pause the automated builds while testers were working, effectively losing the benefit of the frequent feedback from the automated builds. The team went to their management and made the case for a dedicated Cucumber environment.

> ### Seeking Feedback on Partially Completed Work
>
> *The team gathers for an informal review, including a stakeholder.*
>
> *Setting: The team conference room in the library's downtown office, the next morning.*
>
> *(MARK, ROBIN, RAJ, SAM, JESSIE, JANE, and JONAH are sitting around the conference table.)*
>
> *MARK:* I invited Susan to join us in a few minutes. Since we're taking a new approach with BDD, I thought it would be good for her to see where we are at. I wanted to let you know ahead of time that she would be here, so you're not surprised.

I was excited when Raj told me we already had some initial stuff to show on the "happy path" scenario, and since I wanted to take a look, I thought Susan would too.

SAM: Susan is very supportive of our team and usually attends our sprint demos, but isn't it a little risky to be showing things to people outside the team, let alone a key stakeholder? We only started this yesterday. We've barely even started. What if Susan misunderstands and thinks we're already done?

JONAH: We've been quite intentional about what we have to demo today. It will be very obvious that it's not done.

Mark and I made sure Susan knows that what we are showing will look very rough, and we've been very clear that we're mostly looking for feedback of initial exploration at this stage, not approval of finished work.

RAJ: OK, but what if she is disappointed about how little we've done? Like I mentioned to you yesterday?

JONAH: It's possible, but unlikely. Once again, she understands that you are learning something new and that with this early work you may be slower to complete features. However, she was excited to be invited to see something after only a couple days of work, and we saw an opportunity to showcase your learning to her.

MARK: Right, don't be too concerned. Jonah and I had a good talk with Susan yesterday, explaining to her where we're at. As you said, Sam, she's very supportive of what we're doing.

JONAH: Exactly. Mark and I made sure Susan has appropriate expectations for this: Susan knows it's just an informal review, a "check- in," not an end-of-sprint demo.

We're going to review and discuss the happy path scenario, at least as much as we've managed to get done so far. We'll do a quick walk-through of the other, failing, scenarios. And we're going to review the mockups together.

(SUSAN *walks in*)

MARK: Hi, Susan, thanks for joining us; I'm glad you can make it.

SUSAN: *(Sits down at the conference table)* Thanks for inviting me. Hi, everyone.

JONAH: Hi, Susan. Glad you could make it.

As Mark and I mentioned to you, we thought it would be good to show you what we've got so far with the ebook search feature. The team's made some good initial progress already, and we wanted to get feedback from you and Mark early to make sure we're heading in the right direction.

SUSAN: Sounds good to me.

MARK: OK. Raj, can you walk us through what you've got?

RAJ: Of course. Let me walk you through the ebook search feature manually, then I'll show the Cucumber scenarios running.

The test automation runs too fast to demo effectively, so if you are interested in that it will be better to start with the feature file again and go through each step in the browser first so you can see it working for real before you see the steps verify it in an automated way.

SUSAN: Makes sense.

MARK: Yes.

JONAH: Raj, before you walk through it, why don't you and Robin help us understand what we are actually seeing?

ROBIN: Yes! After you paired with Raj to get the rough cut of the pages working and the happy path scenario passing, Raj and I spent the rest of the day writing the real search code. We had some initial tricky technical challenges to overcome with integrating the open-source search framework on top of our ILS, but were able to figure them out and had it working for real by the end of the day.

MARK: So, you'll be showing us the actual ebook search running against our current catalog?

RAJ: Yes, in our integration test environment, which has a copy of the production catalog data. We were able to keep the Cucumber happy path scenario passing as we replaced the hard-coded pages with real data.

SAM: So, you know that scenario still works as we specified yesterday, even though the code changed?

JANE: Yes. Absolutely.

MARK: Good; let's see it.

JONAH: As Raj shows this, keep in mind that the ebook search and results pages are still very rough. At this point we want you to focus on the *way it works* rather than *how* it looks. We'll talk about how it looks after we've had a chance to review how it works, so don't be worried if it seems to be somewhat "bare-bones" now.

SUSAN: Sure. Sounds good.

MARK: OK. Ready, Raj?

Faster Stakeholder Feedback

Teams using BDD have more opportunities to seek feedback. By working on the product one complete example at a time, the product can be "done"—for that set of scenarios—multiple times per day. The work becomes a series of small transformations to support more and more scenarios rather than many scenarios going from not working to working in large batches.

When a system has many things partly working, it can be risky to show it to senior stakeholders—something might behave in unexpected ways. But when a system is fully working, albeit for a limited set of scenarios, it's predictable and safe to share and talk about.

Note, however, that the team was careful to set Susan's expectations that she was seeing work in progress to get a sense of direction, not something complete that would go out to customers. This created a safe context for the team to share the currently working scenarios and to seek feedback from Susan about other scenarios they might not be thinking about yet.

An Unexpected Opportunity

RAJ: Yes. *(Clicking in browser window on projector)*

As you can see, I go to the ebook search page. As Jonah explained, it's very rough at the moment, just a text field and a button. I type "Words of Radiance" into the search box, which is already in our catalog as the scenario comment says, then click the Search button. The results come back, and the catalog entry for *Words of Radiance* is at the top of the search results. As the feature file specified, we have the correct values being displayed for Name, Author, Call Number, and Format.

We're still making it work for other variations in the search terms and results.

ROBIN: It might not seem like much, but there are a lot of new technical things going on behind the scenes to make that search work.

JANE: Yes, and we have much more control over the way the search works with partial matches, as a later scenario highlights.

MARK: It seems much faster than our current search, or is that just because it's in our test environment?

RAJ: You're right. Robin and I noticed this too. It's a welcome side-effect of using this new search framework, and not because we are using our test environment.

The test environment actually runs *slower* than production in all cases. Robin and I ran some initial informal performance tests, and we're seeing an order of magnitude speed increase on our searches using this new approach, even in testing. So, we should see an even faster response in production.

MARK: Well, that's good news!

SUSAN: Yes, I agree. We often get complaints from our library patrons about how hard it is to find things and how long it takes for the search results to come back. This is very encouraging: well done.

ROBIN: Yay!

RAJ: I am very glad to hear you're pleased. We were pleasantly surprised too. We plan to push this to staging later today, since it is almost an exact copy of the production environment, to confirm our performance metrics by running more rigorous performance tests.

SAM: To staging? Won't that cause problems with our final testing for the next release?

RAJ: Good question, Sam. The short answer is, "No, it won't." These changes are completely separate from what we've done for the other release. There's a tiny risk of issues, but we'll be checking it in staging after the push, just to be sure.

Jane?

JANE: Since it's a new page and new code, there's negligible risk of it affecting anything in the current release. I talked about it with Robin and Raj and we all agree the impact is minimal, if anything.

I'm convinced there's a lot of value in pushing it today, even though this is not normally something we would do. I want to see it run in staging and, with Raj and Robin's help, I also want to confirm the performance improvement we're seeing.

Mark, are you OK with this?

MARK: Yeah, I'm happy with the idea, so long as you, Raj, and Robin are OK.

RAJ: Yes, we are. There is minimal risk, and a lot to be learned. It will give us the chance to finish and test our deployment scripts, and make sure all the new components work together smoothly in staging as well as test.

We have often had problems in the past with deploying new things to production, so this will help alleviate some of the technical risk by letting us test the deployment very early.

I've already talked with Brian, who handles our production deployments, and he is happy and ready to work with us. Once it's in staging, you'll all be able to try it.

SUSAN: Excellent. I have an executive directors' meeting at the end of tomorrow and would love to show this to them. They've been waiting years to see us move into digital content, so showing them even this small part will demonstrate that we're making real progress now. They'll be pretty excited about it. Raj, can you email me once it is ready?

RAJ: Yes; we'll make sure everything is working correctly in staging before I email you.

MARK: Sounds good, Raj. We've never had something working we could push out to staging this early in the process. I'll be in Susan's meeting tomorrow, so if you have problems getting it running in staging and think it might not be ready, just let me know, and I'll demo it from test for Susan's meeting. I'll also make sure Susan and I communicate the expectations correctly to the other directors.

Raj, why don't you run the Cucumber scenarios?

RAJ: Of course. Thanks, Mark. *(Typing)*

As you can see, there's not much to show when I run the automated tests. Everything happens so fast that all you really see is that the first scenario is green and the rest of the scenarios are red. These other scenarios are red because we haven't finished implementing them yet.

MARK: But I see some of the steps for the failing scenarios are green, such as "Given I am on the ebook search page" and "When I search for 'Radiance'." Why's that?

JONAH: Good observation, Mark. Those steps are green and passing, even though the overall scenario is failing, because we are reusing steps that are already implemented and working.

SAM: But the overall scenario is red because…?

JANE: Because Raj and Robin haven't yet implemented the final step in the scenario, Sam. So, even though in that scenario it can get to the ebook search page and use the search form they implemented in the happy path scenario, there is still some coding they need to do for the final step to get the book to come back correctly in the search results. Isn't that right?

ROBIN: Yes. Still some more tweaking of the search API that we didn't get a chance to finish yesterday. We hope to get that done right after this meeting, then those other scenarios will pass too.

RAJ: Correct. We don't expect it take long to make the changes. We've already reviewed the scenarios with Jane and understand how it needs to work. In fact, it was Jane who suggested these new scenarios yesterday based on her early testing.

If we get it done and pushed to test this morning, then Jane can review it and make sure we got it right.

JANE: Sure, I've got time this morning. And if it looks good then we'll push it to staging as well for you to review and demo.

MARK: Got it. Sounds good. This is great progress, everyone. Anything else we need to cover?

How Getting to Done More Often Changes All Sorts of Things

Having the system in a stable state creates opportunities around deployment, customer relationships, feedback, and architecture. Things that weren't possible with work in larger batches become possible.

On past projects, Susan wouldn't have engaged with the product so early. She certainly wouldn't have considered showing it in an executive directors' meeting in the first weeks of development. But knowing that the system would behave predictably, albeit for a limited range of scenarios, she could safely show it to senior leaders to give them a better sense of progress than a typical status report would provide.

In the same way, the team was able to safely experiment with their application performance in the production-like staging environment and safely experiment with architectural changes, supported by a safety net of passing scenarios.

Good Agile teams already have this stability at the iteration level or, better yet, the user story level. BDD brings the increment of "done" down to the scenario level. Moreover, the need for scenarios to be represented as automated tests aligns the team around really getting done scenario by scenario.

Legacy System Challenges

JONAH: You've all seen Jessie's email about the UI mockups for this feature. While we have everyone in the room, let's review them before Raj and Robin incorporate the UI designs into this new ebook search feature. Jessie?

JESSIE: Hi, everyone. I printed out the mockups for everyone and stuck them up on the whiteboard here. I've drawn arrows on the whiteboard between the page mockups so you can see the user flows.

(Everyone stands up and walks to the whiteboard to review the mockups.)

MARK: Looks great. Seems very clear.

JESSIE: The layout is almost identical to the general catalog search, though I've taken the opportunity to improve and standardize the styling greatly. It's close visually to what we have now, but having a new feature to work on outside our legacy catalog system has given me the chance to make some good visual improvements.

SUSAN: Yes, it does look much cleaner than our current search page, without looking too different. Why haven't we done this kind of nice restyling for our existing search page?

JESSIE: Hmmmph. I wish I could.

The way the markup and styling are done for our existing site is a bit of a mess. I've inherited a decade of inconsistent changes made by contractors without an overall design vision or style guide. It's almost impossible to make these kinds of changes in our ILS without doing a lot of work and without the risk of breaking everything.

SUSAN: That's unfortunate. No wonder it takes so long to get new features out the door.

ROBIN: And that's just the UI piece, not to mention all the code complexity hidden under the surface. What you see in the browser is just the tip of the iceberg.

JANE: I'll add that not only is it hard to write new features in our current legacy system, it's incredibly hard to test them, too. Everything is so interconnected.

RAJ: With our legacy ILS, it's like that old programming joke about object-oriented systems: "You want a banana so you ask for it, and you get the gorilla holding the banana and the whole jungle as well!"

ROBIN: *(Laughing)* Exactly.

RAJ: This approach Jonah has showed us of building something new *alongside* our existing system gives us just the "testable banana" we are looking for...

JANE: ...without risk of being mauled by the legacy "gorilla."

RAJ: Indeed. I can't imagine us trying to do BDD this way with the legacy gorilla and jungle to deal with too.

Frequent Visibility and Legacy Systems

Adopting BDD with a large legacy system poses challenges that teams working on new systems don't have to deal with. The complexity of a legacy system can make it difficult to transform the system with a series of small changes—any change in one area can break the functionality in another area.

This would seem to prevent frequent visibility. It seems like developers on a legacy system need to make changes in large batches. But there's an alternative approach that fits nicely with BDD.

The library team used a strategy sometimes called *integrate and strangle* to focus on adding new value to a legacy system without having to wrestle with all the complexity of the existing code. They rejected the tendency to rewrite the legacy system, which would have taken them down a road littered with the burning wrecks of failed projects. Instead, they integrated new code and tools with the legacy system to provide valuable new functionality *alongside* the existing system, using BDD with Cucumber for the new features.

In other words, augment existing systems by *extending* them, rather than modifying them, where possible. Wrap them in services, using approaches like REST to isolate your new work from the existing system. Over time, the new code can replace existing behavior and slowly strangle the legacy system. But at every point along the way, the whole system works and adds more and more value. This is far superior to the typical rewrite project where the system remains in an unstable state for months or years simply trying to re-create existing functionality on a new technology, never releasing incremental new value along the way.

Style Guides, Technical Specs, and Other Related Living Documentation

JESSIE: It's been so nice to rethink the design afresh this week and get it the way I want it for this new feature. I've been able to make subtle, but important, changes to the way it looks without being tangled up in all the existing spaghetti code. As you can see, I've used exactly the same examples as the scenarios in our feature file.

Any comments or questions?

SAM: Looks like an improvement to me.

MARK: It looks really nice and matches what we have been talking about. Let's go ahead with it.

JESSIE: This approach will make changing it much easier in the future. You won't notice it on the mockups, but I've also reworked the images so they load faster.

Jonah advised us to annotate some of the important markup elements so we can keep them consistent.

RAJ: Robin and I have been coding up the pages according to these annotations, so we're all agreed on them. Jonah keeps emphasizing striving for consistency in language, design, and code. Having this kind of consistency will really help us with future design work and delivery of new features, too.

ROBIN: Yes, and not just by establishing these kinds of technical patterns and standards to follow, but also by keeping focused on the business language and examples.

RAJ: Robin and I just need to finish implementing the rest of the scenarios for this story and it will be done. We have the rest of today, so I expect we'll have it working completely by this time tomorrow. We have just a few minor search framework tweaks before we take it to test and staging and do some performance and deployment work. Tomorrow we should be able to incorporate Jessie's UI changes.

SAM: We should update the technical documentation on the wiki as part of these changes, right?

RAJ: Yes, correct. Robin and I will set aside a bit of time after we finish the other scenarios to make sure that's done. I'll create a nicer, electronic diagram of the architecture and put it up on the wiki. We'll link to the feature file and build results from our wiki too, so anyone can see the feature file and the passing specs.

SAM: Can I help with those documentation updates?

RAJ: Sure. It would be a big help if you could at least do an initial pass at the updates. Why don't I send you the links and diagram and you let me know when you're ready for me to fill in the details?

SAM: Will do.

MARK: Great. If it looks like you can get the UI changes done and pushed to test and staging before tomorrow morning, let me know. It would be great to demo a completed story in the executive briefing. But don't worry if you run out of time. Either way, this has been very encouraging and enlightening. I look forward to seeing what comes next.

SUSAN: I agree. Good job, everyone. Mark and I will let you know how the demo at tomorrow's executive briefing goes.

Mark, if we're done here let's head back to my office and talk a little about what we want to say at the briefing. I want to make sure we communicate clearly to them what we are learning and what we've accomplished so far.

MARK: Sounds good.

Documentation: Integrated and Living

BDD both contributes to and creates a need for incremental documentation. Growing feature files function as living documentation of the intended (and actual) behavior of a system. Rather than reading an out-of-date requirements document to understand how a system is supposed to work, you can run and read a suite of

Cucumber scenarios that naturally stay in sync with the system (and alert you via failing scenarios when they get out of sync).

Other kinds of documentation need to change incrementally, too. If the system is going to be in a "done" state more often, documentation such as design descriptions and architectural diagrams need to stay in sync with the system in ways they didn't have to when software was only occasionally done and released.

In Chapter 7, "Growing Living Documentation," we flesh out this concept of living documentation more thoroughly.

Team Demos the Finished Story and Discusses Next Steps

Setting: The team conference room in the library's downtown office. Two days after the informal review, and the morning after the executive briefing.

(MARK, ROBIN, RAJ, SAM, JESSIE, JANE, and JONAH are sitting around the conference table.)

MARK: Yes, yesterday's executive briefing went very well. They're used to not seeing anything from us for long periods of time, usually toward the end of our major release, so it was a big positive to be able to show what we've done so far. Plus, since Raj and Robin were able to verify the speed increases and also incorporate most of Jessie's UI changes, it gave us a great story to tell about what we're accomplishing and how it's leading us to big improvements in design and delivery.

SAM: Shouldn't we have waited until we were done, though? After all, in Scrum, aren't we only supposed to demo "potentially shippable product increments?"

MARK: Since they only meet once a month, Susan and I didn't want to wait another month to show our progress.

JONAH: I'm glad you were able to do that, and thanks again for inviting me to the briefing. Mark and Susan did a great job of presenting what everyone has accomplished this week, and everyone in the meeting was excited about the work you've all done this week and what might be coming up.

MARK: Thanks, Jonah.

JONAH: To Sam's point, which is a good one, it's generally better to only show stories that are done, to avoid any misunderstandings about where things are really at. You don't want to be calling things done that aren't. Teams should avoid any confusion about that, but in this case it made sense.

ROBIN: I was just excited to see something that we worked on this week actually make it to staging so quickly and get so much visibility to the organization.

JONAH: Exactly. That's what you need to be focusing on. How about we demo the finished story and acceptance criteria? Mark, would you do the honors, "Mr. Product Owner?"

MARK: Of course. Now that all the UI work is incorporated in it looks great, as well as working great. Raj, could you show the scenarios all passing?

RAJ: And here are all the Cucumber scenarios, all green.

Closing the Loop on the MMF

JANE: So, Mark, will we be deploying this first story to production? We could, if you want.

MARK: Right. It's certainly a "potentially shippable product increment," to use Scrum terminology. We've established that quite clearly. However, it's not a minimum marketable feature, an MMF, yet. Jonah?

JONAH: Yes. What Mark means by MMF is the smallest unit we can deliver that has meaningful value to the people using it. Another way of saying it is that it's the smallest set of functionality that's worth shipping to users. You always want to start by finding a small, high-value slice of the product you can deliver first.

JANE: Are you saying ebook search alone doesn't have any value?

MARK: It does, but probably not enough yet to release it alone. When Susan and I discussed this, we wanted to include borrowing as part of our first MMF. After all, just knowing an ebook is in the catalog but not being able to borrow it isn't really useful to our patrons.

JONAH: From my notes here, the second story that is part of the MMF was written as: "In order to actually read the book, I want to be able to check out an ebook to my Kindle."

MARK: Right. We also had a third, which was: "In order to get more ebooks I want in the library, I want to be able to tell a librarian when searching by title didn't find the book I wanted."

We actually started implementing that as part of the ebook search. I guess I need to do a better job of making the MMFs and stories more visible to us all as we break them down and then work on them.

JONAH: Agreed. Let's regroup about that later today. It would be good to have Sam and Jessie be part of that conversation too, since Sam tends to do some of the product owner work and Jessie is the ScrumMaster. We can figure out together some first steps to getting you all more visibility into your backlog, especially as you transition back into a regular sprint cycle for upcoming work.

RAJ: I'm not sure we would be able to finish this second story as quickly as we did the first. Checking out a Kindle book is very involved, especially if we have to keep track of it and expire it.

JONAH: OK, I suggest we walk through the story together and get an idea of what it involves and whether it warrants splitting into smaller stories.

RAJ: It sounds like this second story may be very complex. I doubt we'll be able to split it.

JONAH: Well, let's see, shall we? I've heard many, many people say they have a large story that couldn't be decomposed into meaningful smaller deliverables, and I haven't found one yet that we couldn't split.

JESSIE: Since that is the next one, I'll do some preliminary sketches of pages and UI flow.

JONAH: OK. Well, why don't we break now? Mark, how about you, Sam, Jessie, and I reconvene in an hour to refine the product backlog in preparation for the next sprint?

MARK: Works for me.

SAM: Sounds good.

JESSIE: Will do.

Avoiding Mini-Waterfalls and Making the Change Stick

Susan and Mark Discuss Progress and Next Steps with Jonah

Setting: Cafeteria.

(SUSAN, MARK, and JONAH are sitting having coffee.)

MARK: I saw a new, much higher, level of team focus this week. More than I've ever seen before, even doing Scrum.

JONAH: That's great. What did you notice that was different this week?

MARK: Well, I'm concerned that in the past the team hasn't had enough visibility into what they needed to do. I often had no idea where they were at. We tried tracking task hours and story burndown charts, but they didn't seem to help much. And it seems like we spend ages in our sprint planning meeting and have a measure of clarity by the end of the first day of the sprint. Then, as the sprint wears on, every day seems to be worse.

Jane would be stressed out because most of the stories would require testing in the last couple of days of the sprint. It put her under a huge amount of pressure.

Also, it seemed that in past sprints Raj and Robin would tend to pull in a bunch of stories at the start of the sprint and start working on them all at once.

Maybe that's why Jane would be so slammed with work at the end. Because all the stories would be in progress at the same time, then get completed at the same time at the end of the sprint?

I've tried encouraging Raj and Robin to just work on one or two at a time, but they tell me they are concerned about not getting them all done in time, so they want to get started on most of them as soon as they can.

This week it was really clear what story everyone was working on. What was different with how we did things this week?

Sam was also much more involved this week. His role seemed a little more fluid and collaborative with the rest of the team, and I noticed the whole team focusing on completing just a few things and getting them done.

JONAH: Do you remember this week how we always discussed examples on the whiteboard or screen where everyone could see them? And how we paid a lot of attention to getting things visible?

MARK: Yes, that was very helpful. It made a big difference.

JONAH: Teams that lack visibility into the work tend to stay siloed, each person working on their own thing. BDD will have trouble thriving in a team environment where it is easier not to collaborate, which is what your prior Scrum implementation has tended to be.

BDD requires focus at multiple levels. You'll notice that we tended to focus on one MMF, then one story, then one scenario at a time. We got one of those parts to the right level of detail before we started coding it, while at the same time we were still refining the rest.

MARK: Right. That was much improved.

JONAH: It's the *privilege of focus*: By not trying to work on everything at the same time, you actually get more done. On the other hand, trying to do BDD with Cucumber in mini-waterfalls like your previous sprints have been will only lead to frustration. You don't want to make this harder than it already is.

SUSAN: I can see how working on small chunks would help Jane. She would be able to avoid having a big batch of testing work at the end of the sprint like she has had in the past.

JONAH: Exactly.

SUSAN: What are some likely challenges you see ahead for the team?

JONAH: Most teams do well for a while, then start to struggle with other challenges after the initial enthusiasm wears off. So, coaching doesn't typically end after the first feature. I fully expect, and you should too, that your team will face some significant challenges in the coming weeks and months.

On the technical front, they will likely have features coming up that will require dealing more with your legacy system. I foresee them needing help with applying design techniques to decouple themselves more from your legacy ILS.

The technical piece is only one part of it. You should expect some pushback soon on the team side of things as they settle back into more of a routine.

MARK: Are you sure? They all seem pretty engaged and fired up to me.

JONAH: Yes, they are today. Old habits of siloing work and not collaborating together as a team will tend to come back. New skills that seemed easier this week when I was here will be more of a struggle as the team members work on applying them themselves.

Specifically, the developers might fall back into taking on too much work in progress and not collaborating with Jane. Sam might back away from the team and revert to writing "requirements" and handing them over to the team rather than actively engaging in feature mining, discovery, and exploration of examples.

The team will likely find it difficult to split some stories, making them think it's better not even to try. They may also get caught up in incidental details of Cucumber as a tool rather than focusing on using it to enable collaboration to get software out the door earlier and more often.

There are other potential issues, but those are some of the most common ones I see.

SUSAN: That bad, huh?

JONAH: It doesn't have to be, but these are problems common to many teams I coach, and not even specific to BDD or Cucumber. Any new approach or discipline takes time to learn, and things usually get worse before they get better and reach a new, higher status quo.

Some basic training and a few days of intensive coaching are a great start and put them ahead of the curve in terms of likelihood for success. However, breaking long-standing habits of little focused interaction between team members can take a while, especially when the pressure of deadlines looms.

I'd encourage you to be patient with them, and don't get discouraged when you see these symptoms. Think of them as learning opportunities for the team rather than failures.

MARK: Will do. Anything else we need to talk about?

JONAH: I can help catch and address any issues early by scheduling a regular remote check-in call with the team once a sprint between now and when I'll return.

SUSAN: Sounds good. I know I've learned a lot this week, and clearly have habits and ways of thinking about software delivery that need changing. Anything else you recommend?

JONAH: One more thing I need to finish off this week is to coach Jessie directly on some of the facilitation skills needed for BDD. She's observed me facilitating the conversations, but she's going to need to practice some of the techniques to help keep the team on track as they move forward. I'll meet with her later today for a one-on-one coaching session and then follow up remotely a couple of times in the coming weeks to practice specific areas she needs to improve.

MARK: Excellent. Thanks for everything you've done over the past few days, Jonah.

JONAH: You're welcome. The team has made great progress.

SUSAN: It's more than just the team. As I've said, we've all learned some important things during your visit. And we've already been able to prove to ourselves and the rest of the leadership that this is able to make a big difference in how we deliver.

MARK: Looking ahead, I expect we'll need you again once the team moves on to the next set of features in a couple of months. I'll set up a follow-up call for the end of next month.

JONAH: Sounds good. I'd recommend you talk together about your next steps at leadership level, what your general expectations are for my coaching going forward, and what specific expectations you might have for my next visit. Is that something you'd have time for in the next week or so?

SUSAN: Yes, that's a good idea. Mark and I could do that early next week. It would help us get our thoughts together about where we want to go next. We'll write up some notes on what we come up with.

JONAH: Great. Would you be OK emailing me your thoughts by the end of next week then? I'll review them and send you any feedback. I want to make sure I have a good understanding of how I can best support your goals, and it will help us to already be on the same page when we talk next month.

Summary

- By dramatically shortening feedback cycles and requiring extensive cross-specialty collaboration, BDD changes how a team works in many different ways.
- By reducing the need for manual, scripted testing, BDD frees testers to do more valuable activities like exploratory testing and collaborating on scenarios.
- As the team completes each scenario, they have the opportunity to get feedback from stakeholders.
- To keep up with a system that's frequently in a "done" state, documentation outside Cucumber features needs to become a living, always-changing thing.
- Because this way of working is so different, pay deliberate attention to growing new skills and building new habits, lest the team become overwhelmed and revert to old ways of working after the initial enthusiasm for BDD wears off.

References

Hendrickson, Elisabeth. *Explore It! Reduce Risk and Increase Confidence with Exploratory Testing*. Raleigh, NC: The Pragmatic Programmers, LLC, 2013.

Chapter 6

Making Scenarios More Expressive

Chapter 3, "Formalizing Examples into Scenarios," covered how to use Cucumber's Gherkin language to express examples of your app's behavior. In this chapter, we look at how to go beyond the basics to create scenarios that are fluent, expressive, and a pleasure to read and write. We'll see some common ways scenarios go wrong and how to fix them.

Feedback About Scenarios

As is often the case with teams new to Cucumber, the library team did reasonably well when working on their first feature or two, but they began to struggle with the expressiveness of their scenarios as they moved to a new area of their domain and involved new team members in writing scenarios. From their initial time with Jonah, they had good reference examples around the book search behavior. Now, they have some less-than-expressive scenarios and reengage Jonah to help them improve.

Team Gets Remote Coaching About Some Struggles They Are Having with Scenarios

Setting: The team conference room.

(ROBIN, JANE, SAM, and JESSIE are sitting around the conference table looking at the screen, where JONAH is videoconferenced in.)

JANE: Hi, Jonah. Can you see us OK?

JONAH: Yes. Coming through loud and clear...

JANE: Great! Thanks for joining us. These remote coaching calls have been really helpful in keeping us on track, but since the last one we've been working on implementing credit card payments for library patrons to be able to pay their fines online, and we've struggled a lot with the scenarios in our feature file.

JONAH: OK, can you show me some examples of your scenarios?

JANE: Sure. Let me share my screen. How about this one? I wanted to get experience writing scenarios, so I thought I would create the ones for the actual credit card processing. I'm happy with it, since it looks a lot like one of the test plans I used to write, but Robin has been struggling to implement it.

```
Scenario: Credit Card Payment Wizard
  When I select Visa for the card type
  And I type in a card number of 4111111111111111
  And I type in a name of John Smith
  And I select 09 for the expiry month
  And I select 2017 for the expiry year
  And I click Next
  And I type in 123
  And I click Next
  And I set billing address to 123 Sunshine Street
  And I set City to Denver
  And I set Zip to 80100
  And I click Next
  And I click Confirm Payment
  And I click Submit
  Then I should see Payment Approved
```

ROBIN: Thanks, Jane. This scenario is a good place to start. I've been working on this one today, and it's not so much that I'm struggling to implement it, it's just that something doesn't feel quite right about it, so we wanted to talk with you, Jonah.

I quickly implemented the "I click" and "I select" steps, which we didn't have before from when we did the ebook search work. I reused them throughout the scenario by naming the HTML elements the same as the button name in the step. So, I've been getting a lot of reuse out of the step names.

I'm concerned that the scenario seems very "wordy." It seems like a lot of "When/And" steps to do something that should be quite straightforward. Do you have any advice?

JONAH: This is a very common scenario style for teams new to BDD, and I think you're right to be concerned about it. Let me suggest a few potential improvements.

First, as you noticed, there are lot of steps here. If I read the scenario as a real sentence, I run out of breath after a few steps. If this was an ordinary English sentence, it would be crying out for some punctuation, which is usually an indication that it's too long, as you said.

From the perspective of growing your domain language, when I see a scenario with so many *And* steps, it usually means there's a higher-level concept missing. In this situation, I ask myself, "How would I summarize these steps using business language?" For example, it's the difference between describing all the incidental detailed steps to actually brew the coffee, such as get the coffeemaker, get the water, pour the water, get the coffee beans, grind the coffee beans, and so on…and saying "Brew me a cup of coffee." What's missing is the higher-level "brewing" concept.

SAM: *(Typing)* Well, how about a scenario like this?

```
Scenario: Update Payment Details
  Given I provide valid payment details
  When I run the payment update
  Then it should run successfully
```

JONAH: That's certainly much simpler, but it seems to me to have gone too far in the other direction. Now it doesn't have any details at all, and I'd encourage you to be wary of scenarios that read like tautologies.

SAM: Tautologies?

JONAH: In logic, a tautology is a statement that can't not be true like, "The sky is either blue or not blue."

Remember, scenarios are examples of the desired behavior of your system. So, if I say, "What's an example of successfully updating your payment details?" and you say, "Well, it's when someone updates their payment details and it's successful," that feels tautological. It doesn't really say anything.

So, I'd want you to flesh out "valid" and "successfully" with examples that actually illustrate what those concepts mean in your system.

SAM: OK, we can try that.

JONAH: To dig a little deeper into Jane's scenario, I'd recommend you try to summarize the steps, perhaps considering a single concept like "credit card details" to include all these steps. Or maybe follow Amazon's approach by combining a couple of concepts, like "credit card" for the card number, name on card and expiration date, and then expanding "billing address" to include all the billing address details. If you decide to do that, you might want to revisit your UX to bring it in line with the concepts you're introducing.

JANE: OK, makes sense. That would certainly simplify it.

JONAH: I'm also concerned that you are putting a lot of the implementation details into the scenario itself. They're better hidden in the step definition code. Putting details like UI buttons in the scenario steps themselves will tend to lead you toward these kinds of long scenario sentences, and over time make your test automation brittle.

ROBIN: Brittle? Isn't a good thing to get all this reuse of the scenario steps? For example, I wrote another scenario and was able to reuse the same steps:

```
Scenario: User has fees and fines
  Given I owe $13.05 in unpaid fees and fines on my library account
  When I Log In
  And I go to the My Account page
  And I click "My Fines"
  And I click "Current"
  Then I should see "You have $13.05 in unpaid fees and fines"
```

JONAH: For scenarios, we care more about clarity and expressiveness than reuse. Normally, we try to avoid duplication in our code, but sometimes, we'll choose to allow some duplication in our steps so each scenario is easy to read and understand.

I'd encourage you to keep implementation details, like clicking on buttons and selecting dropdowns, out of the scenario steps. Focus on the business language. Implementation details belong in the step definition code. You can create helper methods that let you get reuse at the code level in the step definitions.

Think about it from the business perspective: Mark cares less about the names of the buttons than he does about the fine calculations working properly, so we want to emphasize that.

ROBIN: OK; I'll work with Jane and Sam to rework these.

How about this one? I wrote this scenario earlier this week, with Jane and Sam adding the step about unblocking the library card. It runs and passes, but now that I look at it, it does seem to have the kinds of implementation details you were warning us against.

```
Feature: Process fee payment using FP service
  Scenario: Submit to FP credit card payment service
    When I send a payment request to FP
    Then I should get a "200 OK" response
    And I should see an empty list of fines and fees
    And I should see "Charges: $0.00 Deposits: $0.00 Credits: $0.00"
    And I should not see "Library card blocked"
```

JANE: I admit, I didn't understand the "200 OK" step at all, and I don't really know what the "FP service" is, other than it's the third-party service we use to make credit card payments.

JONAH: There seems to be a mix of technical implementation details and business language here. For example, the payment request to FP and the "200 OK" response seem to be more like technical details rather than written in business language. On the other hand, having no fines and fees and no longer having your library card blocked seem important as business logic.

So, yes. I see a number of incidental technical details here. For example, what is the "FP" service? I would take that detail out of the feature file entirely, moving it into the step definition code.

The "200 OK" response is another technical detail. With the rest of the steps, there's probably some incidental details in there, but I'm not sure which ones. It's hard to tell what the scenario is actually supposed to be verifying. For example, what does the step about charges, deposits, and credits mean?

ROBIN: Could you give us an example of what a scenario like these should look like? It would really help to have something to use as a guide.

JONAH: Of course.

How about something more like this? *(Types)* It's not perfect, by any means, but assuming I'm understanding what you're trying to do, it should at least be clearer than what you have now. I'm sure you could improve on it.

```
# Uses 3rd party service (FP), covered elsewhere by integration tests
Scenario: Reinstate deactivated account when fines are fully paid
  Given Bob owes $13.05 in unpaid fees and fines on his library account
  When Bob pays the full amount
  Then there should be no fines and fees
  And Bob's library card should be unblocked
```

What do you notice about this version of the scenario?

ROBIN: Well, it no longer says anything about the implementation. I could completely change the UI or the payment service, and the scenario would stay the same.

JONAH: Yep, it's all about the behavior from a business perspective. What else do you see?

SAM: The bit about "Charges, Deposits, and Credits" is totally gone. Isn't that something from the business perspective?

JONAH: I left out that line because it sounds like it's really about a different behavior than this scenario was illustrating. Maybe it belongs in a scenario for the accounting system, but this one seemed to be about what happens to a patron's library card when their fines are paid off. I try to make each scenario just about one thing.

As you clean up a scenario, the intent of the scenario should become clearer. It's common to learn new things about the system behavior through the conversations that happen around the scenario.

JANE: We want to use the same word every time we talk about a particular domain concept, right?

JONAH: Mmm hmm.

JANE: So, this scenario uses three words to refer to what seems to be a single concept. Are we reinstating, activating, or unblocking the account?

JONAH: Who would know the answer to that question?

JANE: We probably should talk to Mark.

JONAH: Great. This is one of the things I love about concrete examples: they make it clear when you haven't built a common language yet. Remember, the whole point of BDD is to have conversations about examples to clarify those kinds of questions. The goal is a shared understanding of the correct system behavior and then making sure the scenario is as expressive as you can make it.

JANE: OK, we'll loop in Mark and keep working to refine these scenarios. Thanks for the help, Jonah.

JONAH: My pleasure. Talk to you later.

ROBIN and SAM: Bye.

How to Make Your Scenarios More Expressive

In his book *Peak*, psychologist Anders Ericsson points to the importance of powerful mental representations of a domain as a key to expert performance. Expert chess players, for example, think about the positions of the pieces on a chess board differently from novices. The experts see combinations of positions, relative power, lines of force, where the novices see only individual pieces in arbitrary places. This allows the experts to reason more powerfully about where to move next.

Expressive Cucumber scenarios help developers and stakeholders build a mental representation of how the system is intended to behave. The better the representation, the better decisions they'll be able to make about what feature to build next, how to perform exploratory testing, and how to avoid defects, among other things.

Poorly written scenarios can still function as automated tests. They keep you from unknowingly breaking something in the system that used to work, but they squander an opportunity to use scenarios to produce better and better software.

To get expressive scenarios, we need to look at three things: the level of abstraction, the appropriate amount of detail, and the language in the steps themselves.

Finding the Right Level of Abstraction

The same scenario can be described using several different kinds of language. In the previous dialogue, the team wrote scenarios at two extremes. Their first scenario, the version written by Jane, was too low-level. It included implementation details and read like a manual test script. When Sam tried to fix it, he went too far the other way and created what we call a tautological scenario. It abstracted so many details away that it no longer expressed anything meaningful about the behavior (other than telling us that successful behavior should be considered successful).

Avoiding Tautological Scenarios

At one extreme is the tautological scenario, with insufficient detail to illustrate the feature. Sometimes these aren't even a proper example. Clues that indicate a tautological scenario are words in the Then step like *correct* or *successful*, as in the following example:

```
Scenario: Search for a book
  When I search for a book
  Then I should see the correct results
```

When you find yourself writing a tautological scenario, ask yourself, "For example?" After you generate one example, ask, "What's another example?" Tautological scenarios often hide several examples that illustrate different aspects of what *correct* or *successful* mean. It can also be useful to explicitly define terms, as in, "How would I know if I had *correct results*?" and "What would *incorrect results* look like?"

Avoiding Overly Technical Scenarios

At the other extreme is the technical scenario, containing details meaningful only to technical team members and tightly coupled to a particular implementation. For example, this scenario has XPath and CSS selectors and two database tables related by numeric key:

```
Scenario: Search for a book by author
  Given the following Authors:
    | id | name                |
    | 1  | Charles Dickens     |
    | 2  | John Steinbeck      |
    | 3  | Fyodor Dostoyevsky  |
```

```
And the following Titles:
  | id | title               | author_id |
  | 1  | A Tale of Two Cities | 1         |
  | 2  | Crime and Punishment | 3         |
  | 3  | East of Eden         | 2         |
And I'm on "http://www.bookstore.biz/"
When I fill in "Dickens" in "//input[name()='q']"
And I click "#searchButton"
Then there should be 1 "div.book div.title" element
And the page should contain "A Tale of Two Cities"
```

Slightly more readable, but still far from a ubiquitous language, is the scenario written in implementation language like the following scenario. This kind of scenario tends to have words and phrases like *click*, *fill in*, *select*, *page*, and *screen*. Like the technical scenario, these usually are imperative, describing the *actions* one would take to test the scenario rather than the goals these actions support in terms of the business domain.

```
Scenario: Search for a book by author
  Given the following catalog:
    | Title               | Author             |
    | A Tale of Two Cities | Charles Dickens    |
    | Crime and Punishment | Fyodor Dostoyevsky |
    | East of Eden         | John Steinbeck     |
  And I'm on the bookstore home page
  When I fill in "Dickens" in the search field
  And I click "Search"
  Then I should see only "A Tale of Two Cities" in the results
```

The Sweet Spot: A Concrete Domain Example

The most useful Cucumber scenarios express a concrete domain example using the language of the domain, supporting what Eric Evans calls a *ubiquitous language* in *Domain-Driven Design*. Ubiquitous language is the idea that the same language should be used across the whole software development team, from conversations between business and technical people to tests to the code itself. There shouldn't be translation layers of domain concepts between business and technical representations. Growing a ubiquitous language involves effort and commitment but enables a team to have more effective conversations and enables the software to become increasingly expressive of domain concepts. This increase in expressiveness makes the code easier to understand and thus more amenable to change.

Leslie Brooks puts it well when he explains how ubiquitous language benefits his teams:

> The mantra we use is, "If we mean the same thing, we should write it exactly the same way. If we write it the same way, we should mean exactly the same thing."

That gives the developers confidence—if they see the same words, then they know that they know exactly what it means. "I have seen that phrase before. I know what it means, and I can reuse the code that I wrote to implement it." If one word is different, then they know that one-word difference is significant, and they must understand the difference before they implement it.[1]

Ubiquitous language is different from the idea that technical team members should simply adopt the terms used by domain experts. In many cases, domain experts have never had to discuss their domain with the precision required to represent domain concepts in software. This need for precision reveals inconsistencies and ambiguities in the jargon of the domain. Thus, a particular team will need to grow its own ubiquitous language. Many elements of the language will come from existing jargon, but others will emerge from conversation within the team.

A concrete domain example for a book search might look like this:

```
Scenario: Search for a book by author
  Given the following catalog:
    | Title               | Author              |
    | A Tale of Two Cities | Charles Dickens     |
    | Crime and Punishment | Fyodor Dostoyevsky |
    | East of Eden        | John Steinbeck      |
  When I search for "Dickens"
  Then I should see only the following in the results:
    | Title               | Author              |
    | A Tale of Two Cities | Charles Dickens     |
```

This change avoids implementation and technical detail and combines individual actions the user might take on a web page into larger tasks that express meaningful goals in the business domain. There's a nice symmetry between the Given and Then steps, as well, which highlights the behavior of the search operation.

Including the Appropriate Details

Some scenarios are written in good domain language and describe a concrete example but contain excess detail. A large number of quoted strings, numeric values, or table columns can indicate excess detail in a scenario. For example:

```
Scenario: Search for a book
  Given the following catalog:
    | Title               | Author              | Publisher | ISBN       |
    | A Tale of Two Cities | Charles Dickens     | Qualitas  | 1897093594 |
    | Crime and Punishment | Fyodor Dostoyevsky | Dover     | 1936041030 |
    | East of Eden        | John Steinbeck      | Penguin   | 0142000655 |
```

---

1. From personal correspondence with the authors, November 2018.

```
When I search for "Dickens"
Then I should see only the following in the results:
  | Title              | Author          | Format    | Price  |
  | A Tale of Two Cities| Charles Dickens | Paperback | $14.90 |
```

To fix this kind of scenario, challenge the details: "Is it really necessary to know the publisher or ISBN for this example?" Try removing details to see if the scenario still works. Does it still express the example well? Does it differentiate the example from other similar examples?

Exactly what detail is relevant is highly context-specific. Remove too much detail, and you get a tautological scenario that doesn't really illustrate the behavior. The reader needs to bring too much to the table for the scenario to usefully support the mental representation. Leave excess detail in, and the scenario is noisy, requiring the reader to parse out what's important and what's incidental. The best approach is to experiment, to try multiple variations, until you've hit the sweet spot for that unique context.

Sometimes, excess detail gets into scenarios from a well-intentioned desire to increase reuse of step definitions. Reuse has value, but for scenarios, we strongly recommend prioritizing expressiveness over reuse. Use helper methods in your step definitions to increase reuse at that level, but allow for similar yet slightly different steps in your scenarios where it improves expressiveness.

Expressive Language in the Steps

Up to this point, we've talked about scenario language in terms of level of abstraction and amount of detail. The words and grammar you use in the steps themselves also affect your scenarios' expressiveness.

Actors and Verb Tense

We like Given steps to be written in the passive voice. Given describes context, things that just are, so we shouldn't express how they got that way. For example, instead of

```
Given Chandra Khan <chandra@somedomain.com> signs up as a library patron
And Denise Jones <denise@anotherdomain.com> signs up as a library patron
```

we prefer

```
Given the following library patrons:
  | Name          | Email                    |
  | Chandra Khan  | chandra@somedomain.com   |
  | Denise Jones  | denise@anotherdomain.com |
```

We shouldn't care if they just signed up as patrons or if they've been patrons for years. What matters is simply that they're already patrons one way or another by the time we hit the When step.

When steps are about action, so we write them in present tense in the active voice. Someone is doing something that's going to change the state of the system somehow.

There's debate in the Cucumber community about whether the action should be described in the third person ("When the patron does X") or in the first person ("When I do X"). We almost always prefer the first person approach. One of the key functions of scenarios is to build empathy with users so we build products that meet their needs. What better way to empathize with a user than to explicitly put ourselves in her shoes in a scenario, seeing her interactions with the system from her perspective? So, instead of

```
Given Chandra Khan is a library patron
When she logs into her library account
```

we like

```
Given I'm library patron Chandra Khan
When I log into my library account
```

The former has us watching Chandra from the outside. The latter has us imagining what it's like to *be* Chandra using the library system. It's a subtle difference, but we've seen times where that shift causes a team to see something differently and build a better feature.

Be sure that the reader of your feature will be clear who the user is before you take on their voice. We usually establish that context with a step like Given I'm so and so in the Background of a feature or at the start of a scenario.

The one time where we prefer When steps to use the third person is when there are multiple actors and it needs to be clear who's doing what. For example, in a chat application, many scenarios would involve two or more people interacting and could benefit from naming the actors throughout.

Finally, Then steps express an expectation, a preference, for how the state of the system will change after the action in the When step. To make that sense of expectation clear, we like to use the word *should*. Instead of

```
When I pay my outstanding fines in full
Then my account is reinstated
```

use

```
When I pay my outstanding fines in full
Then my account should be reinstated
```

Sometimes, the outcome in a `Then` step is one the user wouldn't like. For example:

```
Scenario: Fines accrue daily
  Given the standard fine is $0.25 per day
  And I've borrowed a standard book
  When I return the book 4 days late
  Then I should be fined $1.00
```

No one really wants to be fined. But they do want their fines to be calculated correctly. So, we like the word *expect* to express expectation, if not preference. So, the `Then` step in the preceding scenario changes to

```
Then I expect to be fined $1.00
```

Along the lines of the first versus third person preference in `When` steps, some people feel strongly about keeping the actor out of the `Then` step, so they'd prefer

```
Then my account should be reinstated
```

to be changed to

```
Then the system should reinstate my account
```

We don't feel strongly about this. If it's more natural in English to express the expectation in terms of what the user sees, do so. If it's more natural to talk about what the system does or how its state changes, do that instead.

Remove the Filler

For some reason, new Cucumber users tend to include filler words in their steps. The classic example is `Given that` when just `Given` would do the job. In the following step, that doesn't do any work:

```
Given that I'm library patron Chandra Khan
```

We can simply delete it. Look for other words that don't earn their space in a step—delete them to focus the reader on the core meaning.

To some, this level of fine-tuning feels excessive. But consider this: Every step will be read many more times than it's written. It's worth a little extra care with our language at writing time to make the reading easier and more pleasant.

Entities and Attributes

We often see steps that look like this:

```
Given a library patron with name "Chandra Khan" and email "chandra@somedomain.com"
```

This step is creating an entity with certain attributes. It's reasonably expressive, but it's long (and it's only going to get longer as we add attributes). We prefer to express steps like this using a key-value table argument:

```
Given a library patron with:
  | Name  | Chandra Khan             |
  | Email | chandra@somedomain.com   |
```

This approach makes it easy for the reader to associate the kind of entity (a library patron) with the two pieces of data in this particular one. (It's also easier to work with in the step definition.)

Notice the colon after `with`. Cucumber doesn't require it, but it's a small touch to make the step more readable for humans, telling the reader to look down to the next line.

Refactoring Scenarios

To improve a scenario written in technical or implementation language, ask, "How would a nontechnical user describe this step?" Consider, "If I implemented this with a completely different technology, what step would describe both implementations?" Look for steps that can be combined into a single domain action. For example, going to the home page, filling in the search field, and clicking the search button could all be considered part of the single action of searching for a book.

When faced with a technical scenario like the earlier example, it can sometimes be useful to refactor through a series of small changes to the language rather than directly to domain language. First, change steps like

```
When I fill in "Dickens" in "//input[name()='q']"
```

to

```
When I fill in "Dickens" in the search field
```

Then, once you have the noise of many of the technical details out of the way, it will be easier to identify the larger domain concepts in the scenario.

It's not always obvious how best to represent a particular example as a Cucumber scenario. While there are some guidelines to follow (such as avoiding technical language), exactly what language is best is partly a matter of style and personal preference. Language style will vary by team and domain. Don't be afraid to try multiple approaches and keep the one you like best. In a new domain or area of an application, we'll often write the same scenario three different ways to see which is more expressive. (Note how we make this decision using concrete examples rather than theoretical arguments about which is best.)

Be careful, though, not to get paralyzed trying to make your features perfect. Your understanding of the domain is always changing and growing. Your skill with Cucumber is growing. And your system is changing every day. Your features will never be perfect, but you can certainly take care with them and make them better.

Good Scenario Titles

Good scenario titles contribute to the readability of a feature. A good scenario title answers the question, "What is this particular example intended to illustrate?" Usually, that's a rule or a rule plus something about the particular variation illustrated by this example.

Remember that the scenario titles need to make sense in the context of the feature title. Don't repeat the feature title in each scenario title.

So, instead of

```
Feature: Ebook Search
  Scenario: Search for a book
```

we'd want to see something like

```
Feature: Ebook Search
  Scenario: By author - Complete last name matches
```

or

```
Feature: Ebook Search
  Scenario: By author - Partial last name matches
```

These scenario titles express what we're doing—searching by author—as well as the particular variation of author search this particular scenario illustrates.

Summary

- Expressive Cucumber scenarios build shared understanding on a team and function as long-term living documentation. Scenarios are read many more times than they're written. Getting the language right is worth spending time on.

- Scenarios should describe concrete domain examples in domain language.

- Avoid tautological scenarios, ones that are abstracted so far from the details of the system that they essentially say, "It's successful when it's successful."

- Avoid overly technical scenarios that contain technical implementation details.
- Include details that are essential for a particular example. Strip out excess detail.
- Use passive voice in Given steps. Write When steps in present tense in the active voice, usually in first person as the user of the system. Use words like *should* or *expect* in Then steps to communicate a preference or expectation for a certain outcome.
- Strip out any filler words in your steps that don't do work.
- Use key-value tables in steps that create an entity.
- Refactor scenarios in small steps. Try two or three alternatives to find the phrasing that works best (using concrete examples!), but don't get hung up trying to make your scenarios perfect.
- Give your scenarios good titles that express what behavior this particular example is illustrating.

References

Ericsson, Anders. *Peak: Secrets from the New Science of Expertise*. Boston: Houghton Mifflin Harcourt, 2016.

Evans, Eric. *Domain-Driven Design: Tackling Complexity in the Heart of Software*. Boston: Addison Wesley, 2004.

Chapter 7

Growing Living Documentation

We've seen how Cucumber can be used to support development of new behaviors in a system, but Cucumber scenarios live longer than the current user story. A suite of Cucumber scenarios is living documentation for the behavior of the system. In this chapter, we explore just what *living documentation* means and why it's better than traditional documentation, we see which documents a Cucumber suite replaces and which documents continue to be useful, and we discuss how to organize and maintain your Cucumber suite to best serve you over the long haul.

What Is Living Documentation, and Why Is It Better?

When we say *living documentation*, there's an implied contrast with "dead" documentation. Typical documentation is dead in two ways:

- There's no direct connection to the product itself
- It gets out of date quickly

Cucumber scenarios are functional documentation, a description of how a system is supposed to behave. This is an area where dead documentation problems are particularly acute. The best "dead" functional documentation is a snapshot of the desired or implemented behavior of a product at a moment in time. But there's no way to tell what's accurate or not—the documentation doesn't alert us when it diverges from the product itself.

And the documentation and product will inevitably diverge. In a complex environment, we can't know in advance exactly what we'll be building and how we'll be building it. Doing the work reveals what needs to be done. So, it doesn't take long for the actual behavior of the product to diverge from the documentation that describes what's going to be built.

Documents rarely go out of date all at once. Thus, people find themselves having to wade through a mix of accurate and inaccurate information to make decisions.

Living documentation is executable. If the behavior of the product changes, the documentation alerts us to the change. Sometimes, the change is intentional, as when adding a new behavior requires a change to existing behaviors. Other times, the change is accidental, a regression defect. Either way, the documentation should tell us so we can respond by correcting the documentation or the behavior.

Living documentation is continuously updated to stay in sync with the system it describes. In fact, one of the signs you've gotten the language and level of abstraction for a scenario right is if the scenario has to change when the behavior it describes changes...but only then. If a new, unrelated behavior breaks an old scenario, there's probably extraneous detail in the old scenario. On the other hand, if adding a new behavior causes you to change how old functionality works, you should have to change the old scenario. If the scenario doesn't have to change, it's probably too abstract and maybe even tautological (see Chapter 6, "Making Scenarios More Expressive").

Cucumber Features and Other Documentation

Cucumber scenarios replace several common kinds of documents. They easily replace requirements specifications and as-built functional documents. Cucumber scenarios describe the intended behavior of the system, both before and after development.

In their role as automated customer-facing tests, Cucumber scenarios also replace detailed test plans, test cases, and test scripts. Cucumber scenarios describe what examples should be tested for a particular behavior or rule. If we know in advance that we want to test a particular case, it deserves a scenario so the team can implement it correctly, building quality in.

Finally, a suite of Cucumber features replaces, or more accurately, removes the need for, traceability documents. The requirements are the tests. Want to know if the system actually does what a scenario says it should? Run the scenario: It will pass or fail.

This is particularly valuable in regulated environments such as medical device development, where an auditor might want to confirm you've thoroughly tested that the system in fact does what the documents say it does. The typical traceability matrix claims this but doesn't actually prove it.

Many other kinds of documents will continue to exist, whether to support collaboration during development, to support maintaining and extending the system later, or to help users use the system effectively. These might include

- Design documents or sketches
- Photos, screenshots, and mockups
- Data dictionaries
- Glossaries
- Support guides
- User guides

Avoid Gherkin in User Story Descriptions

While Cucumber features and scenarios can replace many kinds of documentation, sometimes teams can get a little too excited about Cucumber scenarios and start using them where they don't belong.

Should Cucumber Scenarios Be Used in User Story Descriptions?

Setting: In the hallway during JONAH's next onsite coaching visit.

(JANE and SAM approach JONAH.)

JANE: Jonah, glad I caught you. Sam and I wanted to ask your opinion about something.

Since Gherkin does a good job of formalizing examples, Sam had suggested we start writing the acceptance criteria for our user stories using

Gherkin. We both thought this was a good idea but wanted to get your opinion on it before we proposed it to the rest of the team.

JONAH: I've seen some teams have success with this approach, but I usually recommend against it. It might work for teams that are distributed, where they might need to write things down more before having a conversation about them. For your team, though, you're all collocated and can easily have face-to-face conversations about the acceptance criteria. Save the formalization for the feature file and keep the user stories about conversations. User stories are *told*, not written. If you think of them that way, you'll avoid falling into the trap of thinking you have to write everything down.

SAM: What? Are you saying I shouldn't write anything down?

JONAH: Ah, no. I said don't write *everything* down. I like user stories because they shift the focus from writing to talking, since words are imprecise and written documents aren't as effective for communication as conversations. Keep your user stories lean, focus on the conversations and examples in your acceptance criteria, and augment as necessary with any documents you might feel are helpful, including documents like that one you created for the fines and fees.

SAM: (Laughs) Alright. It's been a long process over these months, but I've learned to trust your recommendations.

There are two situations in which using Gherkin scenarios in user story descriptions seems like a good idea:

- Over time, Cucumber scenarios end up doing the job that you probably previously handled with acceptance criteria bulleted out in your user story descriptions. It might seem logical at this point to start embedding scenarios, written in Gherkin, into your stories.

- Or, maybe you're the first one on your team to take an interest in BDD, and although your team doesn't seem to be ready to automate scenarios, you might want to get them in the habit of using scenarios by just writing them in your stories.

Either way, we don't recommend using Gherkin scenarios. Recall from the definition of BDD in Chapter 1, "Focusing on Value," that BDD is about collaboration around examples before formalizing examples. Don't formalize until you have to. Scenarios aren't intended to replace collaboration. Formal Gherkin scenarios are really a bridge into automation. Until you're thinking about automating, and ultimately, implementing your scenarios, there's no need to go there yet. If you know of scenarios you want to use to illustrate a story in your backlog, simply list them out in freeform language. Provide just enough detail to prompt collaboration, and wait until later to formalize the scenarios into Gherkin. This avoids wasting time with early formalization and, even more important, it leaves room for discussion and learning a bit longer.

The Unexpected Relationship Between Cucumber Features and User Stories

How you organize your Cucumber features and scenarios determines how effectively they act as living documentation. A common mistake is to treat a Cucumber feature as the documentation for a user story.

Organizing Scenarios

SAM: Jane, what about Jessie's suggestion to arrange the scenarios by user story? I suppose that's also a bad idea?

JANE: Yeah, what do you think about that, Jonah?

JONAH: A lot of teams get confused between user stories and feature files. They are not the same thing. I've seen some teams arrange their scenarios by user story, which started out OK but became a maintenance nightmare pretty quickly. So, I'd also recommend against doing that.

JANE: What happened?

JONAH: Well, this team had been very familiar and comfortable with employing user stories for their product planning, so they organized their Cucumber features and scenarios based on them: one Cucumber feature per story.

They had already adopted the practice of describing features similar to how they described their user stories: "In order to __, As a__ I want to __".

This reinforced their conviction that Cucumber features were the same as user stories. Their ScrumMaster convinced the team to organize their scenarios by user story to help her keep track of their progress within each sprint. The team decided to group the feature files into folders, so at the start of each sprint they would create a new folder for the feature files to be worked on in that sprint. It didn't end well.

SAM: How so?

JONAH: Well, by the time they brought me in, they were drowning in feature files and finding it more and more difficult to justify the use of Cucumber as a communication and collaboration tool. A couple of sprints before I came they had decided in their sprint retrospective to try organizing new Cucumber features by higher-level product planning artifacts such as epics and MMFs, but it didn't take away much of the friction.

The new feature files were bigger, containing many more scenarios per feature, but the features described in each feature file seemed unrelated to many of the scenarios they contained. Finally, the sprint-based feature file folder organization scheme continued to feel obfuscating, ad-hoc, and constraining. At this point the team was almost ready to give up on Cucumber altogether.

JANE: I can imagine. Did they? Give up, I mean.

JONAH: They certainly came close, but I talked them back from that ledge. I convinced them to switch to organizing features by functional product divisions rather than by product-planning artifacts like MMFs and user stories. They talked with marketing and other stakeholders and customers and divided their retail website product into business capabilities: browsing the catalog, payment, order placement, catalog management, etc. Within each of these business capabilities, they categorized system functionality into groups of features that supported that capability. They came up with a high-level feature file folder structure, with Catalog Browsing, Payment and Order Placement, Product and Catalog Management, and Order Fulfillment. By that point they had hundreds of feature files and thousands of scenarios, as I recall.

SAM: That must have been a huge amount of work to reorganize all that!

> *JONAH*: It was. But it was important work, keeping their living documentation maintainable. They felt they had unwittingly painted themselves into a corner, so they needed to figure out how to get out of their situation. They set aside capacity each sprint to move scenarios out of the existing sprint-based structure into the new capability-based structure on an as-needed basis, rather than take the productivity hit of migrating all existing feature files immediately.
>
> As they did this, they found it easier to manage the creation of new features and scenarios, communication and collaboration around the new work improved, and it became easier to locate feature files and scenarios that had been created in the past. It took several months, but they eventually migrated all their existing scenarios and removed duplication and confusing tests wherever they found them. As a result of organizing their features this way, using Cucumber started to be fun and useful again.
>
> *JANE*: Wow.

Ephemeral units such as user stories are not a good structure around which to organize features. The reality is that no transient product-planning artifact can ever work well as an ongoing organizational structure for scenarios. The Gherkin format for describing features appears similar to how many teams describe user stories, but they simply are not the same thing. Cucumber features represent living documentation of the behavior of the system.

Cucumber scenarios should be organized around business capabilities—long-lived, natural functional divisions in the product. Organize your scenarios this way, and they'll continue to be useful for the lifetime of the system they describe.

Stable Scenarios

After a scenario is created, should it ever change again? Some teams find themselves in a situation where adding new behaviors to the system requires updating old scenarios to accommodate these new behaviors.

Our rule of thumb is this: When the behavior a particular scenario is illustrating changes in the system, the scenario should have to change to express the new behavior, but if the old behavior hasn't changed, the scenario shouldn't have to change.

If it does, this is a sign the scenario talks about things that are incidental to the behavior it's supposed to be illustrating. For example:

```
Scenario: Fuzzy Match on Title
  Given the following books in the catalog:
    |Title                 |Author          |Publisher         |Date|ISBN            |
    |A Tale of Two Cities  |Charles Dickens |Penguin Classics  |2003|978-0141439600  |
    |Persuasion            |Jane Austen     |Penguin Classics  |2003|978-0141439686  |
    |The Cities Book       |Lonely Planet   |Lonely Planet     |2009|978-1741798876  |
    |The Tale of Despereaux|Kate DiCamillo  |Candlewick Press  |2003|978-0763617226  |
  When I search for books using the phrase: tale cities
  Then the search results should include only:
    |Title                 |Author          |Publisher         |Date|ISBN            |
    |A Tale of Two Cities  |Charles Dickens |Penguin Classics  |2003|978-0141439600  |
```

This scenario includes details about the particular edition of *A Tale of Two Cities* that matches the search query. But the behavior is really just about matching the book title. If, for example, the format of the search results changed to not show the ISBN, this scenario would fail, even though the behavior illustrated by the scenario still works.

Following the recommendations for scenario language in Chapter 6 will help you write scenarios that don't break due to incidental system changes.

Growing and Splitting Features

We like to have the fewest feature files we can so it's obvious where to look for scenarios about a particular behavior. Start with a general feature area, and then split the feature when necessary.

For example, our library team might have a feature about renewals of borrowed items. Any scenarios related to renewals would go in this file. Two situations would cause us to split a feature file:

- Split when backgrounds diverge
- Split when a new domain concept emerges

Split When Backgrounds Diverge

After a feature file gets a handful of scenarios, there are usually one or more Given steps repeated in every scenario. As we discussed in Chapter 3, "Formalizing Examples into Scenarios," these repeated steps can be extracted from the scenarios and moved into a `Background` section near the top of the feature file. This increases the expressiveness of the feature by clearly calling out context common to all the scenarios in the feature and by focusing each scenario on what makes it distinct.

When a new scenario or set of scenarios seem like they'd fit in an existing feature but they don't share the existing `Background`, this is either a sign that steps were moved to the `Background` prematurely or that the new scenarios belong in a separate feature with a different `Background`. An indication it's the latter is if you can name the domain concept that differentiates the new scenarios (that's probably part of your new feature name).

In our renewals feature, the team might have several scenarios related to renewals from the patron's perspective and several from the librarian's perspective. For example, the patron is concerned with actually renewing a book, while the librarian might get a report of frequently renewed books. The `Background` is likely to say something about the current user, so it makes sense for these scenarios to end up in separate features.

Split When a New Domain Concept Emerges

Sometimes a scenario starts in an existing feature, but when you go to name the scenario, you realize it's not really describing the behavior of the thing in the feature name. For example, suppose our library team added a scenario to the renewals feature illustrating how a patron can't renew an item when they have accumulated fines on their account above a certain balance. This might trigger another scenario about how the renewal is allowed after the patron's fines are paid. So far, so good. But what if they add another scenario about the fines accumulated between a book going overdue and becoming renewable? That one isn't really about the renewal behavior; it's really a scenario about fines and belongs in the fines feature. If there's not already a fines feature, this is the time to create it.

Secondary Organization Using Tags

While we prefer long-lived feature areas as the main way of organizing our scenarios, sometimes it's useful to group scenarios in other ways. For example, you might want to run just the scenarios associated with a particular user story, even if they're spread across two or three different feature files. For this, we use tags. In the following example, you can see two scenarios in different feature files both associated with a user story with ID 1234. This story requires changes to the system in different places that are best described in different feature files, but we still want the capability to run all the scenarios associated with that story as we develop and test it.

```
# holds-patron.feature
Feature: Holds - Patron Side

  Background:
    Given I'm a library patron

  @us1234
  Scenario: Placing a hold puts it on my pending holds list
    Given I have no pending holds
    And I'm viewing the book details for "A Tale of Two Cities"
    When I place a hold on the book
    Then my pending holds list should include "A Tale of Two Cities"

# holds-librarian.feature
Feature: Holds - Librarian Side

  Background:
    Given I'm a librarian

  @us1234
  Scenario: Notify librarians to move books to the hold shelf
    Given "A Tale of Two Cities" is in stock
    When patron Richard Lawrence places a hold on "A Tale of Two Cities"
    Then I should receive the following hold notification:
      | Title        | A Tale of Two Cities |
      | Author       | Dickens, Charles     |
      | Call Number  | 823.8                |
      | Borrower     | Richard Lawrence     |
      | Shelve Under | LAWR                 |
```

Boolean logic is possible with tags. So, for example, if you have a large suite to run on a build server, you might want to do a quick smoke test before you take the time to run the full suite. You could configure your build to run a handful of scenarios tagged @smoke first. Then, if those pass, you could run the scenarios that do not have the @smoke tag. You wouldn't have to run the @smoke scenarios twice.

The following are other common uses of tags:

- Tagging scenarios that require a piece of infrastructure like an email server that might not be present in every environment, so they run only in the appropriate environments.

- Tagging scenarios that are particularly slow so you can run the fast scenarios more often.

- Tagging scenarios that are unreliable or "flickery" so you can handle them differently (and, hopefully, fix them over time).

- Tagging the scenarios associated with the behavior you're currently working on so you can run just those more often.

Tags can easily get out of control and make features noisy for the reader. We recommend starting without them. Then, as you notice you want to run different sets of scenarios together, identify the simplest way to group them and experiment with that tag for a while. Don't try to anticipate all the tags you might need in advance.

Structure Is Emergent

The right organization of a Cucumber suite won't be obvious up front. As the system grows, the best way to represent the behavior of the system will change and emerge. Don't try to anticipate the perfect structure, and don't worry if it never feels perfect. Living documentation of a changing system will always be in flux along with the system—just try to make sure it's accurate and understandable at all times.

Summary

- Traditional documentation is "dead" in the sense that there's no direct connection to the product itself and it can get out of date quickly.

- Living documentation is executable and continuously updated.

- A suite of Cucumber scenarios can serve as living documentation about the behavior of a system.

- A Cucumber suite replaces some documentation and lives alongside other documentation. For example, design documents, support guides, and user guides might still be necessary.

- Avoid using Gherkin scenarios in user story descriptions. Wait to formalize scenarios until closer to development and then directly in a feature file.

- Organize scenarios into features based on long-lived business capabilities, not based on ephemeral product-planning units like user stories. Cucumber features do not correspond directly to user stories.

- For sustainability, scenarios should be stable. They should need to change only when the behavior they illustrate changes.

- Try to have a small number of feature files. Split when `Backgrounds` diverge or when a new domain concept emerges that deserves its own feature.

- Tags are useful for secondary organization, but wait to use them until you really need a way to group scenarios across features; they can make your features noisy.

- As you add scenarios and features, refactor your suite so that it always represents an accurate and understandable description of the system's current behavior.

Chapter 8

Succeeding with Scenario Data

Scenarios need data—that's what makes them concrete examples rather than abstract specifications.

Chapter 6, "Making Scenarios More Expressive," covered getting the right detail—the right data—in a particular scenario. But as your suite of Cucumber features grows, it's no longer just about getting the right detail in each scenario. To preserve maintainability, speed, and expressiveness across the suite, you must pay attention to your larger approach to data.

In this chapter, we look at principles and strategies for handling data as your Cucumber suite grows.

Issues with Data Across Scenarios

Setting: ROBIN's desk

RAJ: (Walking into the cubicle) Hey, Robin. I've got a scenario that's randomly failing, and I can't figure out why.

ROBIN: Let's check it out.

RAJ: It's this one: *(Shows laptop)*

```
Scenario: Ebook Borrowing Is Handled on amazon.com
  Given an available ebook
  When I try to borrow the book
  Then I should be redirected to my Amazon account
```

Most of the time, it works the way I expect. But maybe 1 in 20 runs, it fails as if the behavior really stopped working. When I manually test it, it works fine.

ROBIN: Show me the behavior the scenario's about.

RAJ: OK. So, I go to the ebook search page and search for a book I know is available on Kindle. Let's do *A Tale of Two Cities*. I click on Borrow, and it takes me over to the page to borrow the book at Amazon, just like it should.

ROBIN: Maybe we should run it a bunch of times until we get it to fail again.

RAJ: OK. *(Typing)*

RAJ and ROBIN: *(Watching as the scenario runs)*

ROBIN: It happens really fast, but it seems like the page on Amazon changes. Which book are you trying to borrow?

RAJ: *(Looking at the code)* I'm just grabbing the first available Kindle book. It doesn't really matter which book it is.

ROBIN: It doesn't seem like we'd want our scenarios dealing with different examples every time they run. But before we touch that, let's see if we can figure out which book is failing and why.

RAJ: Good idea. I'll just have it write out the title and author of the selected book to the console so we can see it. *(Typing)* OK, let's run it. *(Typing and waiting)*

RAJ: So far, so good. *(Waiting)* OK, that one failed.

ROBIN: *(Laughing)* "*Book* by Author McBookface". I'm pretty sure that's not real. Why do we have a fake book in there showing as available?

RAJ: I didn't put that one there, did you?

ROBIN: No, but I kind of wish I had.

RAJ: Let me search for "McBookface" in the project. *(Typing)* There. This scenario adds that book to the catalog…and never removes it.

(Searches library catalog on his computer) Look, we have 437 copies of it.

ROBIN: *(Laughing)* Yeah, that's not good.

RAJ: It's one of the scenarios Jane wrote to cover the existing book management capability: *(Showing Robin the scenario)*

```
Scenario: Books show up right away when added
  Given I'm a librarian
  When I add the following new ebook to the catalog:
    | Title       | Book              |
    | Author      | Author McBookface |
    | Format      | Mobi              |
    | Call Number | FIC MCBOOKFA A    |
    | ISBN        | 123-4-56-788910-0 |
  Then it should appear in the available ebooks list
```

ROBIN: *(Looking up the step definition code on her computer)* You know what's funny about this one? It only actually worked once.

RAJ: *(Tilts his head quizzically)*

ROBIN: See? *(Pointing)* The first time it ran, the book got created, and it didn't get cleaned up. So, the next time, even if the book didn't get created successfully, the old one is going to make the Then step pass.

RAJ: Hmm. I bet we've done something like that in one of our scenarios somewhere. Good catch.

ROBIN: Yeah, we'll have to keep an eye out for that.

RAJ: I think we're getting to the point where we need to agree how to handle test books.

ROBIN: And probably test patrons, too.

RAJ: Mmm hmm. Why don't I set up a meeting with the whole team, and we'll talk through this issue and figure out what to do?

ROBIN: Good idea. Maybe see if you can get Jonah to call in, too. I'm sure we're not the first ones to have this issue.

RAJ: Right. Watch for the meeting invite. *(Leaves)*

Characteristics of Good Scenarios

Across domains, the scenarios created by teams experiencing success with BDD and Cucumber show some common characteristics. The scenarios that such teams create are typically

- Independent
- Repeatable
- Researchable
- Realistic
- Robust
- Maintainable
- Fast

Let's address each of these concerns in turn and look at their implications for scenario data creation and management.

Independent

Avoid any sort of coupling between scenarios. The most common cause for this is state that persists between scenarios. This can be accidental, or worse, by design. For example, one scenario adds a record to a database and subsequent scenarios depend on the existence of that record. This might work but will create a problem if the scenarios are run separately, in a different order, or in parallel.

In the dialogue, Raj had an unreliable scenario due to accidental coupling with another scenario created by Jane. One scenario was leaving behind database records that randomly caused another scenario to fail.

Scenarios need to be completely *independent*. Scenarios that are isolated from each other can be run in any order. They don't have dependencies that cause failures for reasons unrelated to the actual behavior being verified. Have each scenario set up its own context (i.e., in the Given steps) with everything it needs to run successfully.

Repeatable

Scenarios must be *repeatable*: when run over and over again, they should produce identical results. A team cannot trust scenarios that give different results each time—passing sometimes and failing others. *Tests that cannot be trusted get ignored. Ignored tests do not provide the value that justifies developing them in the first place.*

A scenario's job is to reliably describe how your system works. When you discover a nondeterministic scenario, find out what the problem is and fix it.

Teams often create nonrepeatable scenarios by failing to control the state of the system in their Given steps or by failing to clean up their mess after each scenario. They assume that the system is in the right state without ensuring that it is; thus, their scenarios become unpredictable, as we saw in the dialogue.

Researchable

When a scenario fails, determining the cause of the failure needs to be as easy as possible. That is, scenarios must be *researchable*. It can be very frustrating to know that a scenario is failing, not because the functionality is unimplemented or because existing functionality has changed but because of some other unknown reason.

The easiest way to get researchability is to use specific assertions that will provide informative failure messages. Rather than "expected true, got false," you want a message like, "Expected title 'A Tale of Two Cities', got 'Book'."

To improve researchability, we sometimes include assertions in Given steps so that if the starting state for a scenario is wrong in some way, the scenario fails early and with a clear error message.

Raj and Robin temporarily added logging to their scenario to troubleshoot the unexpected failure. This is fine when troubleshooting a single scenario, but informative assertions would be a much more effective solution across their Cucumber suite.

Realistic

Use test data values in your scenarios that are as close to real business data as possible. Make them *realistic*, avoiding the common tendency to utilize unrealistic developer-facing test data values such as User A, User B, Sample Address, User Name, and so on (like Author McBookface in the dialogue). Work closely with your testers, users, customers, and whoever else might be helpful in finding meaningful data for your scenarios.

Your scenarios should maximize collaboration, learning, and discussion by focusing attention on the real details of the actual business domain. Unrealistic data only gets in the way of this goal. Use real data in your scenarios where possible, or sanitize it by changing certain details if it contains sensitive or private information. The need for real data will force developers to discuss the scenarios with domain experts and testers. It will help the team identify significant data variations and drive toward a deeper shared understanding of the nuances of the business domain and the problems your team is trying to solve.

In the dialogue, using unrealistic test data actually hid a bug. The two scenarios Raj and Jane wrote suggest that in the library's system, it's possible to add an ebook to the catalog that appears to be available but isn't actually on Amazon. A discussion about which book to add to the catalog in Jane's scenario would likely have revealed that books in the catalog need to match books on Amazon.

Robust

Your team must be able to trust its tests. Being *robust* means that scenarios do not break easily due to unrelated things in the team's software ecosystem. The underlying step definitions should be written with a level of care that makes them progressively more immune to other things needing to change, such as development environments, build scripts, database schema changes, or database locations. Tests should not break for infrastructure reasons and should avoid unintended side effects on the surrounding infrastructure. Be especially wary of audit tables, database replication, triggering emails, and so on. Tests that fail for the wrong reasons undermine a team's confidence in the capability of the tests to verify their application's behavior correctly. When scenarios fail for the wrong reasons, fix them; don't just rerun them until they pass.

One common source of fragility in scenarios is a dependency on the system time. Leap years, holidays, and weekends can break scenarios. To make date-heavy scenarios robust, decouple your application from system time and set the time explicitly in your scenarios.

Another common source of fragility is sharing systems with other users, such as running the Cucumber suite on a system also used for manual exploratory testing, as we saw in the dialogue in Chapter 5, "Frequent Delivery and Visibility." Avoid this by dedicating a system to your automated tests and maintaining control over its data.

Maintainable

Maintainability means that tests can be easily understood and modified by someone after they are written—even if it's not the same person who wrote them. Scenarios, and the underlying step definition code that supports them, are code too and should be treated as such. Dale Emery writes, "*Any* time spent puzzling out the meaning and significance of a test is maintenance cost…these 'trivial' maintenance costs add up, and they kill test automation efforts."[1]

---

1. Dale H. Emery, "Writing Maintainable Automated Acceptance Tests," http://dhemery.com/pdf/writing_maintainable_automated_acceptance_tests.pdf

He also notes that:

"Test automation is software development. This principle implies that much of what we know about writing software also applies to test automation…much of the cost of software development is maintenance—changing the software after it is written. This single fact accounts for much of the difference between successful and unsuccessful test automation efforts…successful organizations understand that test automation is software development, that it involves significant maintenance costs, and that they can and must make deliberate, vigilant effort to keep maintenance costs low."[2]

Fast

Scenarios should run as *fast* as you can make them run. Scenarios that run quickly maximize the amount of feedback that the tests will provide and will increase the pace of your ability to code and deliver features. Fast tests get run more often.

Scenarios that interact with databases (versus in-memory operations) are notorious for slowness due to the cost of performing the database operations. Speed is more difficult to achieve with database-dependent scenarios, but it's worth the investment. The same is often true with services and other outside dependencies. If your scenarios run slowly, they'll be run less often and the value they provide will quickly diminish.

That said, speed is sometimes in conflict with the other characteristics. For example, you might find yourself doing the same setup over and over again to keep your scenarios independent. We recommend paying attention to the other characteristics first and turning your attention to speed only after building a decent suite of scenarios. Learn what independent, reliable, maintainable scenarios look like for your application. Then, measure where the performance bottlenecks are and optimize for speed.

Agreeing on the Data Approach

(RAJ, ROBIN, SAM, and JANE are in the conference room. JONAH is videoconferenced in.)

RAJ: Thanks for coming, everybody. Robin and I had an experience yesterday that made us realize we needed to agree how to handle test data in our scenarios.

---

2. Ibid.

I was struggling to debug a scenario that randomly failed. I'd written the scenario to just grab the first available ebook—which I now know was a bad idea. Anyway, Robin and I discovered another scenario from Jane that was creating a fake ebook Amazon didn't have. My scenario sometimes picked up that fake ebook instead of a real one and then failed when trying to borrow it.

So, I wanted to get us together so we can agree how to handle test data consistently and keep our scenarios from becoming unmaintainable or unreliable.

ROBIN: Obviously, the simplest thing is for each scenario to create the data it needs.

RAJ: …and clean it up.

ROBIN: Right. Jane's scenario wasn't just creating a fake book, it was leaving the fake book in the test database.

RAJ: We found over 400 copies of the book, in fact.

ROBIN: Which had a funny side effect. The scenario really only tested what it claimed to test the first time it ran. Even if you changed the Given step, the Then step would still pass because of a copy of the book left over from a previous run. We're watching for that issue in other scenarios now.

JANE: I can see how leaving those books in the test database would be a problem, but how do I clean them up?

RAJ: Hmm. That's a good question. If we delete the book after the assertion in the Then step, it won't always get deleted. If the assertion fails, the code stops.

JONAH: You're right, Raj. A Then step isn't the place to do cleanup. You may remember, when I first got you going with Cucumber I mentioned hooks, but you didn't have a need for them at the time. A hook is a method that can run before or after every scenario. The After hook is a good place to do cleanup because it runs even when the scenario fails.

So, one way to handle this is to keep a collection of IDs of books to delete. When you create a book, add the ID to that collection. In the After hook, go through the collection and delete all the matching books.

RAJ: OK, we'll check that out.

JANE: Robin said every scenario should create its own data, but a lot of our scenarios don't do that. I mean, really, they can't. We don't control the books on Amazon, for example.

ROBIN: True. And I guess some data could be expensive to set up, even if we control the database. Jonah, how do we handle this?

JONAH: What do you do now with Amazon data?

ROBIN: We make sure to use examples we know are in the system.

JONAH: OK. Sometimes, it's useful to have data with certain characteristics that already exist in the system rather than trying to create it all every time. Ideally, you have some shared examples you can all refer to.

RAJ: How do we keep that from making scenarios hard to debug?

JONAH: I'll often put assertions in my `Givens` so if the data I expect isn't there, they fail right away.

SAM: This sounds like something I can help with. I can come up with a set of standard books with different characteristics.

JANE: I already have quite a few test books for my manual testing, so I can help you.

JONAH: That's a great thing to do. Be careful, though, not to get ahead of yourself. You don't need data for things you don't have scenarios about, so don't try to create a complete test data set. Find just enough examples for your existing scenarios. Then, grow it as you add more scenarios and need more data.

SAM: Should we come up with some standard patrons, too?

JONAH: Do your scenarios require it?

RAJ: We have some scenarios with adults and some with children, but we really don't make a lot of distinctions about patrons. We just say, `Given I'm a library patron` or `Given I'm a juvenile patron`.

JONAH: Then I wouldn't go there yet. But keep an eye out to see if your patrons get more complicated. If you start having multiple `Givens` in a `Background`, especially with tables, that's a signal you might want to start naming them.

RAJ: So, as we refactor the scenarios to use the new data, how do we make sure we don't accidentally break them?

JONAH: I recommend starting with your Then steps. Change those to expect the new data. They'll fail, of course, which is what you want. Then, work backward, changing the steps until it all works. Many people naturally want to go Given first, but the other way fits the test-first mindset better.

RAJ: OK. So, Robin and I will start refactoring scenarios to create and clean up their own data. Sam and Jane will get us some shared test data, especially for things we don't control like books on Amazon. And we'll integrate those into the scenarios as you get them ready.

ROBIN: Are we just focusing on that now? We still have the stories in the sprint.

JONAH: You can do this refactoring slowly. Fix scenarios when they break. Do the new ones right, and update the ones around the edges of the new stuff you're working on. Eventually, you'll get them all switched over.

ROBIN: OK, good.

RAJ: Alright. I think we all know what we need to do. Thanks, everybody, for joining on short notice. Bye, Jonah.

JONAH: Bye.

Sharing Data

Scenario-specific data has the big advantage of keeping scenarios independent and clean, but it can be slow, verbose, and difficult to manage. Many teams eventually begin to feel overwhelmed by all the different clumps of diverse scenario data they need to work with, and it can become a data management nightmare. To prevent this, look for opportunities to consolidate scenario-specific data into shared or common data for some or all scenarios for a particular feature where possible.

In the dialogue at the beginning of the chapter, Raj ran into an issue from the wrong kind of shared data. One scenario created data and another used it—in his case, accidentally. But that's not what we're talking about when we say shared data. We don't mean dependent scenarios. The right kind of shared data would be something like a few well-understood examples of typical and atypical books used to illustrate behavior across many scenarios.

Adopting the practice of actively seeking out shared data buried in scenario-specific data will drive important team conversations about meaningful distinctions in the data, increase the overall level of understanding about the business domain, reduce the volume and complexity of the test data, and simplify data cleanup logic.

Certain data is clearly shared: seed or default data like lists of states and countries, for example. There's no good reason to explicitly create this data for each scenario. (Unless your application is concerned with managing lists of states and countries. But if you're spending your time on *that* application, you might have bigger problems than managing test data.)

When working with shared test data, there's a strong tendency for this data to become bloated, fragmented, and disorganized if just anyone can add to it. To avoid this, we highly recommend that someone on the team play the role of *test data curator* for the shared data. This role is responsible for working with the rest of the team to ensure that the shared test data is consistent, expressive, documented, and sufficient for the team's needs.

Sam and Jane took this job in the previous dialogue. They'll come back to the team with some examples of books with particular characteristics, and the conversation that ensues will create shared understanding about the domain and the distinctions that matter in it.

When to Share Data

Other data is specific to your domain and could be either scenario-specific or shared. When does it make sense to go shared?

- When a shared `Background` step performs data setup for all, or many of, the scenarios in a feature file

- When most of the data you are providing for each scenario has little to do with the specific behavior the scenario describes and you want to draw attention away from the shared data

- When you have standard domain-specific test data, such as

  - A commonly used list of standard medical providers in a health-insurance _system

  - A list of test products and promotions used to drive purchases for an online retailer's ecommerce website

  - Important date ranges (such as effective dates or expiration dates) related to insurance policy documents

  - Weather and terrain conditions for a fire simulation package

Many teams employ a combination of shared and scenario-specific data. As they start to see similar data repeated across scenarios multiple times, they discuss it with the tester and domain expert and then refactor it out by consolidating and standardizing it as shared data.

Raising the Level of Abstraction with Data Personas

In some domains, shared data is more complicated than just a single book. A scenario might require dozens of different things set up in a particular way. To elegantly solve this problem, we like to use what we call *data personas*.

In user experience design (UXD), a persona is a concrete description of the type of user for whom the team is developing the application. They're used to build user empathy and shared understanding of users by team members.

We extend the persona concept into data personas. Data personas are simply known, shared, and named collections of data. They may be typical users or UXD personas, or they may be things like a standard store or weather model.

For example, Richard coached a team working on a system to help university researchers manage labs and research animals. Most of their features had lengthy Background sections with tables to set up each researcher, their offices, their labs, their animals, and so on. From an independent scenario perspective, they were correctly setting up and tearing down the appropriate data for each scenario. However, these complex Background sections made the features difficult to read and understand. And over time, this introduced an increasing amount of friction into their development efforts as they worked on each new feature. Adopting data personas as shared data solved this problem.

To start with, the team introduced the persona of Jennifer the University Researcher, who had a particular office in a particular building, a lab adjacent to her office, and a particular set of research animals. Deborah, also a researcher, had multiple labs and multiple sets of research animals for studies with different dates. John was a research assistant, without an office of his own, who contributed to Deborah's lab work.

Once they defined these personas, they were able to say simply, `Given I'm Jennifer` or `Given I'm Deborah`, and all the relevant data would be set up in a single step.

Of course, this works only if everyone on the team knows what it means to be Jennifer or Deborah in a scenario. We've seen collocated teams make posters for their personas with all the relevant details. Distributed teams could document this in a wiki page or on an intranet, but we find such documentation becomes invisible and gets out of sync with the scenarios. Instead, we recommend documenting the personas in your Cucumber suite with what we call *glossary scenarios* along the lines of

```
Feature: Data Persona Definitions

  Scenario: Jennifer the researcher
    When I'm Jennifer
    Then I should have only the following office:
      | Room Number | AB 123 |
    And I should have only the following lab:
      | Room Number | AB 124 |
    And I should have the following research animals:
    # etc.
```

The `Then` steps in this scenario would examine the shared data about Jennifer and actually assert that it's defined correctly. This makes the definition of the persona visible and robust. If someone changes the data behind the scenes to make their scenario pass, the glossary scenario will break, revealing a conversation the team needs to have about their shared data.

Sometimes, creating your own test objects to support your scenarios can be a lot of manual work. There are many frameworks and tools available that can ease this burden. The factory_bot library (https://github.com/thoughtbot/factory_bot) is a popular Ruby example.

Data Cleanup

Remember to keep your scenarios independent. Make sure each scenario has the test data it needs and cleans up its own mess.

The best cleanup strategy varies with context. In the previous dialogue, the library team planned to try a simple strategy of tracking books created in each step definition and deleting them in an `After` hook. We like this as a starting point because it's fast and easy to understand.

As the test data grows, however, this might no longer be the best strategy. Some teams choose to drop and re-create a database, truncate tables, roll back transactions, or even put the database on a file system like ZFS that can roll back after each scenario. The best choice depends on your needs and your technology.

Summary

- As your suite of scenarios grows, managing test data will be increasingly challenging.
- Good scenarios are
    - Independent—They can be run separately or in any order
    - Repeatable—They run the same way every time
    - Researchable—When they fail, it's clear why
    - Realistic—The data looks like the real world
    - Robust—They don't break from small changes in the environment
    - Maintainable—They can be easily understood and modified
    - Fast—They take as little time to run as possible
- Create shared data for things common to many scenarios.
- Use data personas to easily refer to complicated shared data.
- Ensure that every scenario cleans up any data it creates.

Reference

Emery, Dale H., "Writing Maintainable Automated Acceptance Tests": http://dhemery.com/pdf/writing_maintainable_automated_acceptance_tests.pdf

Chapter 9

Conclusion

By now, you've gotten a glimpse into what it looks like for a typical Agile team to get started with BDD. You've seen the differences between good and bad scenarios. You've learned how to take your first steps toward automating scenarios, and you've seen some of the challenges you can anticipate as you become more advanced—organizing a large suite of scenarios and dealing with complicated scenario data. Better yet, you know some strategies for overcoming those challenges.

A Final Check-in with the Team

Setting: The team conference room.

(SUSAN, MARK, ROBIN, JANE, and SAM are sitting around the conference table looking at the screen, where JONAH is videoconferenced in.)

JONAH: Hi, everyone! Happy New Year! So, what's been happening in the last nine months since we talked?

SUSAN: Hi, Jonah! Well, a few weeks ago we successfully pushed out our fourth major release, with a bunch of new exciting features. I'm really happy with how everything has gone. It's been our best year yet.

MARK: To give a bit more detail, the executive team has been super happy with the improvements in productivity, and our Net Promoter Score for the application is well above average now, compared to painfully low this time last year. We've even won an award from a library journal

---

because of the improvements reported by our library patrons. I'll let Raj tell you the story about our legacy system.

RAJ: Right. Through the new development work, we've actually been able to decouple some key application capabilities—both new and old—away from legacy. And we made some modularity improvements and simplifications to the legacy codebase too.

It's been difficult and tedious in places, and we've still got a long way to go, but I'm pretty happy with how it's been progressing. The approaches you taught us have helped a lot.

We've been able to start applying BDD with Cucumber in other projects and introducing it to other teams, which has kept me busy. I'm glad you taught us to take it slow at the start with a team, like you did with us; otherwise, I'd probably have given up with some of the teams!

SAM: Raj has been a big help. Jessie moved over to another team a couple of months ago, but together she and I started a community of practice around BDD. We've seen quite a bit of interest and have been able to help the other teams get better at collaborating because of what we learned on this project. We've also been helping teams at our new office as they've come on board.

RAJ: Since this approach led us to release more frequently, we realized how inefficient and slow our deployment pipeline was, so we've made some significant improvements, with continuous deployment for the new components and more automation for legacy releases. Robin did a lot of that work.

JONAH: I'm so glad to hear all that! Sounds like you have many positives. I'm sure there's been some struggles too?

MARK: We've certainly had more than our fair share of challenges, especially around management changes and our recent hiring spree in adding ten new junior developers to the org these last few months. It's become clear that this new way of working maybe isn't always for everyone, and some people take longer to get on board than others. With some of them working remotely, we've had to adapt some of our practices as we've grown. And legacy is still slowing us down more than I'd like, though it's much better than this time last year, for sure.

SAM: I haven't had to spend nearly as much time ramping up these new hires on library processes and how the software works as I would have in the past without Cucumber. And Jane and Robin have done a great job of getting them up to speed with Cucumber and our new way of working, not that it feels that new anymore.

JANE and ROBIN: Thanks, Sam!

JANE: I'm much happier now that I can focus more on exploratory testing. Bug rates are way low now, since talking through examples as part of development helps us identify issues before they show up in code. Plus, the shift in my role with this team has freed me up to provide testing guidance to the other teams, especially with Jessie and Sam's support through the community of practice. Robin and I even ran our first internal open space conference last month, and we were able to share a lot of our learning that way.

ROBIN: It was a blast! The energy level was pretty high. Even Sam ran a session on BDD for BAs. Right, Sam?

SAM: Absolutely, it's probably fair to say BDD is more the "new normal" for us now. I couldn't imagine going back to how it was before.

If you've already started with BDD as you've read the book, we hope you've begun to experience a different kind of collaboration, with multiple roles working together around concrete examples to build just the right behavior for your customers. Remember to keep that focus on collaboration first and test automation a distant second.

If you're about to get started, remember the slow lane from Chapter 2, "Exploring with Examples." You don't need to change everything at once. Just pick a single user story to practice with each sprint. Slowly learn how to do BDD well in your context, and then expand. Take your time.

If even that sounds overwhelming, start even smaller: Just use examples more in your conversations about your product. That one simple practice will make your collaboration better. Automation can come later.

Thanks for reading. Go make great software together!

Index

VIDEO TRAINING FOR THE **IT PROFESSIONAL**

LEARN QUICKLY
Learn a new technology in just hours. Video training can teach more in less time, and material is generally easier to absorb and remember.

WATCH AND LEARN
Instructors demonstrate concepts so you see technology in action.

TEST YOURSELF
Our Complete Video Courses offer self-assessment quizzes throughout.

CONVENIENT
Most videos are streaming with an option to download lessons for offline viewing.

Learn more, browse our store, and watch free, sample lessons at
informit.com/video

Save 50%* off the list price of video courses with discount code **VIDBOB**

*Discount code VIDBOB confers a 50% discount off the list price of eligible titles purchased on informit.com. Eligible titles include most full-course video titles. Book + eBook bundles, book/eBook + video bundles, individual video lessons, Rough Cuts, Safari Books Online, non-discountable titles, titles on promotion with our retail partners, and any title featured as eBook Deal of the Day or Video Deal of the Week is not eligible for discount. Discount may not be combined with any other offer and is not redeemable for cash. Offer subject to change.

Photo by izusek/gettyimage

Register Your Product at informit.com/register

Access additional benefits and **save 35%** on your next purchase

- Automatically receive a coupon for 35% off your next purchase, valid for 30 days. Look for your code in your InformIT cart or the Manage Codes section of your account page.

- Download available product updates.

- Access bonus material if available.*

- Check the box to hear from us and receive exclusive offers on new editions and related products.

Registration benefits vary by product. Benefits will be listed on your account page under Registered Products.

InformIT.com—The Trusted Technology Learning Source

InformIT is the online home of information technology brands at Pearson, the world's foremost education company. At InformIT.com, you can:

- Shop our books, eBooks, software, and video training
- Take advantage of our special offers and promotions (informit.com/promotions)
- Sign up for special offers and content newsletter (informit.com/newsletters)
- Access thousands of free chapters and video lessons

Connect with InformIT—Visit informit.com/community

the trusted technology learning source

Addison-Wesley • Adobe Press • Cisco Press • Microsoft Press • Pearson IT Certification • Prentice Hall • Que • Sams • Peachpit Press

 Pearson